Juno and the Paycock

A Tragedy

Sean O'Casey

Samuel French – London

New York – Sydney – Toronto – Hollywood

ISBN 0 573 012148

JUNO AND THE PAYCOCK

Produced at the Royalty Theatre, London, on the 16th November 1925, with the following cast of characters:

"Captain" Jack Boyle	Residents in the Tenement	*Arthur Sinclair*
Juno Boyle, his wife	Residents in the Tenement	*Sara Allgood*
Johnny Boyle (their children)	Residents in the Tenement	*Harry Hutchinson*
Mary Boyle (their children)	Residents in the Tenement	*Kathleen O'Regan*
"Joxer" Daly	Residents in the Tenement	*Sydney Morgan*
Mrs Maisie Madigan	Residents in the Tenement	*Marie O'Neill*
"Needle" Nugent, a tailor	Residents in the Tenement	*J. A. O'Rourke*
Mrs Tancred	Residents in the Tenement	*Kitty Kirwan*
Jerry Devine		*David Morris*
Charlie Bentham, a school teacher		*Eric Page*
An Irregular Mobilizer		*Barney Mulligan*
Two Irregulars	(one)	*E. T. Kennedy*
A Coal-block Vendor		*Edmund O'Grady*
A Sewing Machine Man		*Christopher Steele*
Two Furniture-Removal Men	(one)	*Edmund O'Grady*
Two Neighbours		*Joyce Chancellor* *Mollie Mackay*

SYNOPSIS OF SCENES

ACT I

The living apartment of a two-roomed tenancy of the Boyle family, in a tenement house in Dublin

ACT II

The same

ACT III

The same

A few days elapse between Acts I and II, and two months between Acts II and III.

During Act III the curtain is lowered for a few minutes to denote the lapse of one hour.

Period of the play, 1922.

JUNO AND THE PAYCOCK

ACT I

SCENE—*The living apartment of a two-room tenancy occupied by the Boyle family, in a tenement house in Dublin.*

On the R *is a door leading to the street. Above the door* R *is a window looking into the street. On the* C *back wall is a window. To* R *of the window is a dresser with crockery; to* L *of the window a curtained alcove containing a bed. On the* L *wall up stage is a door leading to another room. Below this door is the fireplace. On the mantelpiece is an alarm clock, lying on its face. On the wall, over the mantelpiece, is a picture of the Blessed Virgin; beneath the picture on the mantelpiece is a small red bowl; the bowl is filled with oil, and in the oil a lighted wick floats. This votive light must be always plainly visible. In* C *of the room is a kitchen table, with chairs, one at the back, and one at each end of the table. On the table is a small mirror, a newspaper spread out at one end, and breakfast things at the other end. A well-worn armchair stands beside the fireplace. There is a pan in the fender and a teapot on the hob. A long-handled labourer's shovel is leaning against the side of the dresser.*

When the CURTAIN *rises,* JOHNNY BOYLE *is sitting crouched in the armchair beside the fire. He is a thin, delicate fellow, younger than Mary; his face is pale and drawn; there is a tremulous look of indefinite fear in his eyes. The left sleeve of his coat is empty. When he walks he has a slight halt.*

MARY *with her jumper off—it is lying on the back of a chair—is arranging her hair before a tiny mirror perched on the table. Beside the mirror is stretched out the morning paper which she looks at when she isn't gazing into the mirror. She is a well-made and good-looking girl of twenty-two. Two forces are working in her mind—one, through the circumstances of her life, pulling her back; the other, through the influence of books she has read, pushing her forward. The opposing forces are apparent in her speech and her manners, both of which are degraded by her environment, and improved by her acquaintance—slight though it be—with literature. The time is early forenoon.*

MARY (*looking at the paper*) On a little bye-road, out beyant Finglas, he was found.

(MRS BOYLE *enters by the door* R; *she has been shopping and carries a small parcel in her hand. She is forty-five years of age, and twenty years ago she must have been a pretty woman; but her face has now assumed that look which ultimately settles down upon the faces of the women of the working-class: a look of listless monotony and harassed anxiety, blending with an expression of mechanical resistance. Were circumstances favourable, she would probably be a handsome, active and clever woman)*

Mrs Boyle. Isn't he come in yet?

Mary. No, mother.

Mrs Boyle (R) Oh, he'll come in when he likes; strutting about the town like a paycock with Joxer, I suppose. (*She puts the parcel on the table*) I hear all about Mrs Tancred's son is in this morning's paper. (*She crosses behind Mary, takes off her hat and black shawl, and flings them on the bed in the alcove*)

Mary. The full details are in it this mornin'; seven wounds he had—one entherin' the neck, with an exit wound beneath the left shoulder-blade; another in the left breast penethratin' the heart, an' . . .

Johnny (*springing up from the fire*) Oh, quit that readin', for God's sake! Are yous losin' all your feelin's? It'll soon be that none of yous'll read anythin' that's not about butcherin'!

(Johnny *goes quickly into the room* L)

Mary (*looking after Johnny*) He's getting very sensitive, all of a sudden.

(Mrs Boyle *comes down to the table* R)

Mrs Boyle. I'll read it myself, Mary, by an' by, when I come home. Everybody's sayin' that he was a Die-hard—thanks be to God that Johnny had nothin' to do with him this long time. . . . (*She opens the parcel and takes out some sausages, which she places on a plate*) Ah, then, if that father o' yours doesn't come in soon for his breakfast, he may go without any; I'll not wait much longer for him. (*She takes the plate of sausages from the table, goes over to the dresser, and puts them in the bottom cupboard*)

Mary. Can't you let him get it himself when he comes in?

Mrs Boyle. Yes, an' let him bring in Joxer Daly along with him? Ay, that's what he'd like, an' that's what he's waitin' for—till he thinks I'm gone to work, an' then sail in with the boul' Joxer, to burn all the coal an' dhrink all the tea in the place, to show them what a good Samaritan he is! But I'll stop here till he comes in, if I have to wait till tomorrow mornin'. (*She goes over and sits beside the fire*)

Voice of Johnny (*inside*) Mother!

Mrs Boyle. Yis?

Voice of Johnny. Bring us in a dhrink o' wather.

Mrs Boyle. Bring in that fella a dhrink o' wather, for God's sake, Mary.

Mary (*still before the mirror, arranging her hair*) Isn't he big an' able enough to come out an' get it himself?

Mrs Boyle (*getting up from the fire, going to the dresser and filling *a glass with water*) If you weren't well yourself, you'd like somebody to bring you in a glass of water.

(MRS BOYLE *goes in with water to the room* L, *and returns and sits down by the fire*)

Isn't it terrible to have to be waitin' this way! You'd think he was bringin' twenty poun's a week into the house the way he's going on. He wore out the Health Insurance long ago, he's afther wearin' out the unemployment dole, an', now, he's thryin' to wear out me! An' constantly singin', no less, when he ought always to be on his knees offerin' up a Novena for a job!

MARY (*tying a ribbon, fillet-wise, around her head*) I don't like this ribbon, ma; I think I'll wear the green—it looks betther than the blue.

MRS BOYLE (*poking the fire viciously*) Ah, wear whatever ribbon you like, girl, only don't be botherin' me. I don't know what a girl on strike wants to be wearin' a ribbon round her head for or silk stockin's on her legs either; it's wearin' them things that make the employers think they're givin' yous too much money.

MARY. The hour is past now when we'll ask the employers' permission to wear what we like.

MRS BOYLE. I don't know why you wanted to walk out for Jennie Claffey; up to this you never had a good word for her.

MARY. What's the use of belongin' to a Trades Union if you won't stand up for your principles? Why did they sack her? It was a clear case of victimization. We couldn't let her walk the streets, could we?

MRS BOYLE. No, of course yous couldn't—yous wanted to keep her company. Wan victim wasn't enough. When the employers sacrifice wan victim, the Trades Unions go wan betther be sacrificin' a hundred.

MARY. It doesn't matther what you say, ma—a principle's a principle.

MRS BOYLE. Yis; an' when I go into oul' Murphy's tomorrow, an' he gets to know that, instead o' payin' all, I'm goin' to borry more, what'll he say when I tell him a principle's a principle? What'll we do if he refuses to give us any more on tick?

MARY. He daren't refuse—if he does, can't you tell him he's paid?

MRS BOYLE. It's lookin' as if he was paid, whether he refuses or no.

(JOHNNY *appears at the door* L)

JOHNNY. I was lyin' down; I thought yous were gone. Oul' Simon Mackay is thrampin' about like a horse over me head, an' I can't sleep with him—they're like thunder-claps in me brain! The curse o'—God forgive me for goin' to curse!

MRS BOYLE. There, now; go back an' lie down agen, an' I'll bring you in a nice cup o' tay.

JOHNNY. Tay, tay, tay! You're always thinkin' o' tay. If a man was dyin', you'd thry to make him swally a cup o' tay!

(JOHNNY *goes back to the room* L)

MRS BOYLE. I don't know what's goin' to be done with him. The bullet he got in the hip in Easter Week was bad enough, but the bomb that shatthered his arm in the fight in O'Connell Street put the finishin' touch on him. I knew he was makin' a fool of himself. God knows I went down on me bended knees to him not to go agen the Free State.

MARY. He stuck to his principles, an', no matther how you may argue, ma', a principle's a principle.

VOICE OF JOHNNY (*in the room* L) Is Mary goin' to stay here?

MARY (*shouting*) No, I'm not going to stay here; you can't expect me to be always at your beck an' call, can you?

VOICE OF JOHNNY. I won't stop here be myself!

MRS BOYLE. Amn't I nicely handicapped with the whole o' yous! I don't know what any o' yous ud do without your ma. (*At the door* L, *to Johnny*) Your father'll be here in a minute, an' if you want anythin', he'll get it for you.

JOHNNY. I hate assin' him for anythin'. . . . He hates to be assed to stir. . . . Is the light lightin' before the picture o' the Virgin?

MRS BOYLE. Yis, yis! The wan inside to St Anthony isn't enough, but he must have another wan to the Virgin here!

(JERRY DEVINE *enters hastily by the door* R. *He is about twenty-five, well set, active and earnest. He is a type, becoming very common now in the Labour Movement, of a mind knowing enough to make the mass of his associates, who know less, a power, and too little to broaden that power for the benefit of all.*

MARY *seizes her jumper, and runs hastily into the room* L)

JERRY (R, *breathless from speed*) Where's the Captain, where's the Captain, Mrs Boyle?

MRS BOYLE (*sitting at the fire; turning to look at Jerry*) You may well ass a body that: he's wherever Joxer Daly is—dhrinkin' in some snug or another.

JERRY. Father Farrell is just father stoppin' to tell me to run up an' get him to go to the new job that's goin' on in Rathmines; his cousin is foreman o' the job, an' Father Farrell was speakin' to him about poor Johnny an' his father bein' idle so long, an' the foreman told Father Farrell to send the Captain up an' he'd give him a start—I wondher where I'd find him?

MRS BOYLE (*getting up and crossing to Jerry*, R) You'll find he's ayther in Ryan's or Foley's.

JERRY. I'll run round to Ryan's—I know it's a great house o' Joxer's.

(JERRY *rushes out of the door* R.
MRS BOYLE *crosses over to the fire again and sits in the chair, in an agitated state*)

MRS BOYLE (*piteously*) There now, he'll miss that job, or I know for what! If he gets win' o' the word, he'll not come back till evenin', so that it'll be too late. There'll never be any good got out o' him so long as he goes with that shouldher-shruggin' Joxer. I killin' meself workin', an' he sthruttin' about from mornin' till night like a paycock!

(*The footsteps of* "CAPTAIN" BOYLE *and* JOXER *are heard coming upstairs, outside the door* R. "CAPTAIN" BOYLE *is singing in a deep, sonorous voice, "Sweet Spirit, hear my Prayer"*. MRS BOYLE *lifts her head and listens; she rises from her seat, goes and stands listening behind the table*)

BOYLE (*outside the door* R, *singing*) Sweet Spirit, hear me prayer! Hear . . . oh . . . hear . . . me prayer . . . hear, oh, hear . . . Oh, he . . . ar . . . oh, he . . . ar . . . me . . . pray . . . er!

JOXER (*outside*) Ah, that's a darlin' song, a daaarlin' song!

(MRS BOYLE *goes to the alcove, backstage* L, *and sits on the bed so that the curtains hide her from view.*
"CAPTAIN" BOYLE *comes slowly in*, R. *He is a man of about sixty; stout, grey-haired and stocky. His neck is short, and his head looks like a stone ball that one sometimes sees on top of a gate-post. His cheeks, reddish-purple, are puffed out, as if he were always repressing an almost irrepressible ejaculation. On his upper lip is a crisp, tightly cropped moustache; he carries himself with the upper part of his body slightly thrown back, and his stomach slightly thrust forward. His walk is a slow, consequential strut. His clothes are dingy, and he wears a faded seaman's cap with a glazed peak*)

BOYLE (*to Joxer, who is still outside*) Come on, come on in, Joxer; she's gone out long ago, man. If there's nothing else to be got, we'll furrage out a cup o' tay, anyway. It's the only bit I get in comfort when she's away. 'Tisn't Juno should be her pet name at all, but Deirdre of the Sorras, for she's always grousin'.

(JOXER *steps cautiously into the room by the door* R. *He may be younger than "Captain" Boyle, but he looks a lot older. His face is like a bundle of crinkled paper; his eyes have a cunning twinkle; he is spare and loosely built; he has a habit of constantly shrugging his shoulders with a peculiar twitching movement, meant to be ingratiating. His face is invariably ornamented with a grin*)

JOXER (R) It's a terrible thing to be tied to a woman that's always grousin'. I don't know how you stick it—it ud put years on me. It's a good job she has to be so ofen away, for (*with a shrug*) when the cat's away, the mice can play!

BOYLE (*with a commanding and complacent gesture*) Pull over to the fire, Joxer, an' we'll have a cup o' tay in a minute.

JOXER. Ah, a cup o' tay's a darlin' thing, a daaarlin' thing—the cup that cheers but doesn't . . .

(MRS BOYLE *cuts Joxer's speech short by springing suddenly out of the alcove, and stands angrily between Boyle and Joxer, glaring from one to the other. Both are stupefied*)

MRS BOYLE (*with sweet irony—poking the fire, and turning her head to glare at Joxer*) Pull over to the fire, Joxer Daly, an' we'll have a cup o' tay in a minute! Are you sure, now, you wouldn't like an egg?

JOXER. I can't stop, Mrs Boyle; I'm in a desperate hurry, a desperate hurry.

MRS BOYLE. Pull over to the fire, Joxer Daly; people is always far more comfortabler here than they are in their own place.

(JOXER *makes hastily for the door.* BOYLE *stirs to follow him; thinks of something to relieve the situation—stops, and says suddenly*—"Joxer!")

JOXER (*at the door, ready to bolt*) Yis?

(BOYLE *crosses in front of Mrs Boyle to Joxer* R, *gets close to him and speaks meaningly*)

BOYLE. You know the foreman o' that job that's going on down in Killesther, don't you, Joxer?

JOXER (*puzzled*) Foreman—Killesther?

(MRS BOYLE *is standing staring at them; she is* LC *and listens to them quietly, but with an ominous glare in her eyes. They are trying to deceive her, but she sees through them*)

BOYLE (*with a meaning look*) He's a butty o' yours, isn't he?

JOXER (*the meaning of Boyle dawning on him*) The foreman at Killesther—oh yis, yis. He's an oul' butty o' mine—oh, he's a darlin' man, a daarlin' man.

BOYLE. Oh, then, it's a sure thing. It's a pity we didn't go down at breakfast first thing this mornin'—we might ha' been working now; but you didn't know it then.

JOXER (*with a shrug*) It's betther late than never.

BOYLE. It's nearly time we got a start, anyhow; I'm fed up knockin' round, doin' nothin'. He promised you—gave you the straight tip?

JOXER. Yis. "Come down on the blow o' dinner," says he, "an' I'll start you, an' any friend you like to brin' with you." Ah, says I, you're a darlin' man, a daaarlin' man.

Boyle. Well, it couldn't come at a betther time—we're a long time waitin' for it.

Joxer. Indeed we were; but it's a long lane that has no turnin'.

Boyle. The blow up for dinner is at one—wait till I see what time 'tis. (*He goes over to the mantelpiece, and gingerly lifts the clock*)

(Mrs Boyle *is standing* LC *watching the movements of Boyle and Joxer*)

Mrs Boyle (*watching Boyle*) Mind now, how you go on fiddling with that clock; you know the least little thing sets it astray.

Boyle (*with the clock in his hand, paying no attention to Mrs Boyle*) The job couldn't come at a betther time; I'm feelin' in great fettle, Joxer. I'd hardly believe I ever had a pain in me legs, an' last week I was nearly crippled with them.

Joxer. That's betther an' betther; ah, God never shut wan door but he opened another!

Boyle (*looking at the clock*) It's only eleven o'clock—we've lashing of time. (*He puts the clock carefully back on the mantelpiece, crosses in front of Mrs Boyle, over to Joxer, and stands beside him,* L) I'll slip on me moleskins after breakfast, an' we can saunther down at our ayse. (*He goes over to the dresser, takes up the shovel, and returns to the side of Joxer, displaying the shovel*) I think, Joxer, we'd betther bring our shovels.

Joxer. Yis, Captain, yis; it's betther to go fully prepared an' ready for all eventualities. You bring your long-tailed shovel, an' I'll bring me navvy. We mighten want them, an', then agen, we might: for want of a nail the shoe was lost, for want of a shoe the horse was lost, an' for want of a horse the man was lost—aw, that's a darlin' proverb, a daarlin' . . .

(Mrs Boyle, *in an angry way, suddenly rushes towards Joxer.* Joxer *hurriedly runs out by the door* R. Mrs Boyle *shuts the door with a bang.* Boyle, *pushed aside in the rush, goes back to the dresser, leaving the shovel back where he got it.* Mrs Boyle, *in a raging temper, crosses quickly to* L *and busies herself with the fire*)

Boyle (*apologetically*) We won't be long pullin' ourselves together again, when I'm workin' for a few weeks.

(Mrs Boyle *takes no notice*)

The foreman on the job is an oul' butty o' Joxer's; I have an idea that I know him meself. (*Silence*) . . . There's a button off the back o' me moleskin trousers. . . . If you leave out a needle an' thread I'll sew it on meself. . . . Thanks be to God, the pains in me legs is gone, anyhow!

Mrs Boyle (*with a burst*) Look here, Mr Jacky Boyle, them yarns won't go down with Juno. I know you an' Joxer Daly of an oul' date, an', if you think you're able to come it over me with them fairy tales, you're in the wrong shop.

BOYLE (*at front of the dresser, coughing subduedly to relieve the tenseness of the situation*) U-u-u-ugh!

MRS BOYLE. Butty o' Joxer's! Oh, you'll do a lot o' good as long as you continue to be a butty o' Joxer's!

BOYLE. U-u-u-ugh!

MRS BOYLE. Shovel! Ah, then, me boyo, you'd do far more work with a knife an' fork than ever you'll do with a shovel! If there was e'er a genuine job goin' you'd be dh'other way about —not able to lift your arms with the pains in your legs! Your poor wife slavin' to keep the bit in your mouth, an' you gallivantin' about all the day like a paycock!

BOYLE. It ud be betther for a man to be dead, betther for a man to be dead.

MRS BOYLE (*ignoring the interruption*) Everybody callin' you "Captain", an' you only wanst on the wather, in an oul' collier from here to Liverpool, when anybody, to listen or look at you, ud take you for a second Christo For Columbus!

BOYLE. Are you never goin' to give us a rest?

MRS BOYLE. Oh, you're never tired o' lookin' for a rest.

BOYLE. D'ye want to dhrive me out o' the house?

(MRS BOYLE *goes from the fireplace, crosses rapidly to dresser;* BOYLE, *fearfully getting out of her way, comes down stage* RC. MRS BOYLE *takes the breakfast things from the dresser—bread, sugar, etc.— and arranges them on the table. She does all in an angry way*)

MRS BOYLE. It ud be easier to dhrive you out o' the house than to dhrive you into a job. Here, sit down an' take your breakfast— it may be the last you'll get, for I don't know where the next is goin' to come from.

BOYLE. If I get this job we'll be all right.

MRS BOYLE. Did ye see Jerry Devine?

BOYLE (*testily*) No, I didn't see him.

MRS BOYLE. No, but you seen Joxer. Well, he was here lookin' for you.

BOYLE. Well, let him look!

MRS BOYLE. Oh, indeed, he may well look, for it ud be hard for him to see you, an' you stuck in Ryan's snug.

BOYLE. I wasn't in Ryan's snug—I don't go into Ryan's.

MRS BOYLE. Oh, is there a mad dog there? Well, if you weren't in Ryan's you were in Foley's.

BOYLE. I'm telling you for the last three weeks I haven't tasted a dhrop of intoxicatin' liquor. I wasn't in ayther wan snug or dh'other—I could swear that on a prayer-book—I'm as innocent as the child unborn!

(MRS BOYLE *goes to the dresser, takes out the sausages from the cupboard underneath, crosses to the fire, puts them on the pan, and starts to cook them.* BOYLE *crosses to back of the table)*

MRS BOYLE. Well, if you'd been in for your breakfast you'd ha' seen him.

BOYLE (*suspiciously*) What does he want me for?

MRS BOYLE. He'll be back any minute an' then you'll soon know.

BOYLE (*starting to the door* R) I'll dhrop out an' see if I can meet him.

MRS BOYLE (*catching him by the shoulder*) You'll sit down an' take your breakfast, an' let me go to me work, for I'm an hour late already waitin' for you.

BOYLE. You needn't ha' waited, for I'll take no breakfast—I've a little spirit left in me still!

MRS BOYLE (*releasing him, and moving away* L) Are you goin' to have your breakfast—yes or no?

BOYLE (*too proud to yield*) I'll have no breakfast—yous can keep your breakfast. (*Plaintively*) I'll knock out a bit somewhere, never fear.

MRS BOYLE. Nobody's goin' to coax you—don't think that. (*She vigorously replaces the pan and the sausages in the press, and returns to the fire)*

BOYLE. I've a little spirit left in me still.

(JERRY DEVINE *enters hastily by the door* R, *looks around and sees Boyle)*

JERRY. Oh, here you are at last! I've been searchin' for you everywhere. The foreman in Foley's told me you hadn't left the snug with Joxer ten minutes before I went in.

MRS BOYLE. An' he swearin' on the holy prayer-book that he wasn't in no snug!

BOYLE (*to Jerry*) What business is it o' yours whether I was in a snug or no? What do you want to be gallopin' about afther me for? Is a man not to be allowed to leave his house for a minute without havin' a pack o' spies, pimps an' informers cantherin' at his heels?

JERRY (R) Oh, you're takin' a wrong view of it, Mr Boyle; I simply was anxious to do you a good turn. I have a message for you from Father Farrell: he says that if you go to the job that's on in Rathmines, an' ask for Foreman Mangan, you'll get a start.

BOYLE (*standing to* L *of Jerry*) That's all right, but I don't want the motions of me body to be watched the way an asthronomer ud watch a star. If you're folleyin' Mary aself, you've no pereeogative to be folleyin' me. (*Suddenly catching his thigh*) U-ugh, I'm afther gettin' a terrible twinge in me right leg!

MRS BOYLE (*near the fire*) Oh, it won't be very long now till it travels into your left wan. It's miraculous that whenever he scents a job in front of him, his legs begin to fail him! Then, me bucko, if you lose this chance, you may go an' furrage for yourself!

JERRY. This job'll last for some time too, Captain, an' as soon as the foundations are in, it'll be cushy enough.

BOYLE (*dolefully*) Won't it be a climbin' job? How d'ye expect me to be able to go up a ladder with these legs? An', if I get up aself, how am I goin' to get down agen?

MRS BOYLE (*viciously*) Get wan o' the labourers to carry you down in a hod! You can't climb a laddher, but you can skip like a goat into a snug!

JERRY. I wouldn't let meself be let down that easy, Mr Boyle; a little exercise, now, might do you all the good in the world.

BOYLE. It's a docthor you should have been, Devine—maybe you know more about the pains in me legs than meself that has them?

JERRY (*irritated*) Oh, I know nothin' about the pains in your legs; I've brought the message that Father Farrell gave me, an' that's all I can do.

MRS BOYLE (*catching him by the shoulder and pulling him towards the table*) Here, sit down, an' take your breakfast, an' go an' get ready; an' don't be actin' as if you couldn't pull a wing out of a dead bee.

BOYLE. I want no breakfast, I tell you; it ud choke me afther all that's been said. I've a little spirit left in me still.

(MRS BOYLE *roughly pulls him past her to* L, *and pushes him towards the door* L)

MRS BOYLE. Well, let's see your spirit, then, an' go in at oncest an' put on your moleskin trousers.

BOYLE (*halting at the door* L) It ud be betther for a man to be dead. U-ugh! There's another twinge in me other leg! Nobody but meself knows the sufferin' I'm goin' through with the pains in these legs of mine.

(BOYLE *goes into the room* L)

MRS BOYLE (*putting on her hat and coat which she takes from the bed in the alcove*) I'll have to push off, now, for I'm terribly late already; but I was determined to stay an' hunt that Joxer, this time.

(MRS BOYLE *hurries out by the door* R.
JERRY *is standing at the* R *end of the table as* MARY *comes in by the door* L. *She is evidently going out, for she wears her coat, and is putting on her hat*)

JERRY. Are you going out, Mary?

MARY. It looks like it when I'm putting on my hat, doesn't it?

JERRY. The bitther word agen, Mary.

MARY. You won't allow me to be friendly with you; if I thry, you deliberately misundherstand it.

Jerry. I didn't always misundherstand it; you were ofen delighted to have the arms of Jerry around you.

Mary. If you go on talkin' like this, Jerry Devine, you'll make me hate you!

Jerry. Well, let it be either a weddin' or a wake! Listen, Mary, I'm standin' for the Secretaryship of our Union. There's only one opposin' me; I'm popular with all the men, an' a good speaker—all are sayin' that I'll get elected.

Mary. Well?

Jerry. The job's worth three hundred an' fifty pounds a year, Mary. You an' I could live nice an' cosily on that; it would lift you out o' this place an' . . .

Mary. I haven't time to listen to you now—I have to go.

(Mary *crosses towards the door* R, *in front of the table;* Jerry *meets her half-way* C)

Jerry (*appealingly*) Mary, what's come over you with me for the last few weeks? You hardly speak to me, an' then only a word with a face o' bittherness on it. Have you forgotten, Mary, all the happy evenin's that were as sweet as the scented hawthorn that sheltered the sides o' the road as we saunthered through the country?

Mary. That's all over now. When you get your new job, Jerry, you won't be long findin' a girl far betther than I am for your sweetheart.

Jerry. Never, never, Mary! No matther what happens, you'll always be the same to me.

Mary. I must be off; please let me go, Jerry.

Jerry. I'll go a bit o' the way with you.

Mary. You needn't, thanks; I want to be by meself. (*She tries to pass*)

Jerry (*catching her arm*) You're goin' to meet another fella; you've clicked with someone else, me lady!

Mary. That's no concern o' yours, Jerry Devine; let me go!

Jerry. I saw yous comin' out o' the Cornflower Dance Class, an' you hangin' on his arm—a thin lanky strip of a Micky Dazzler, with a walkin'-stick an' gloves!

Mary (*protestingly*) You're hurtin' me arm! Let me go, or I'll scream, an' then you'll have the oul' fella out on top of us!

Jerry. Don't be so hard on a fella, Mary, don't be so hard.

Boyle (*appearing at the door* L *in wide moleskin trousers*) What's the meanin' of all this hillabaloo?

Mary. Let me go, let me go!

Boyle. D'ye hear me—what's all this hillabaloo about?

Jerry (*plaintively*) Will you not give us one kind word, one kind word, Mary?

Boyle (*loudly*) D'ye hear me talkin' to yous? What's all this hillabaloo for?

Jerry. Let me kiss your hand, your little, tiny, white hand!

Boyle. Your little, tiny, white hand—are you takin' leave o' your senses, man?

(Mary *breaks away and rushes out of the door* R)

(*To Jerry*) This is nice goin's on in front of her father!

Jerry (*turning and speaking viciously to Boyle*) Ah, dhry up, for God's sake!

(Jerry *follows Mary out of the door* R)

Boyle (L *of the table, standing speechless for a moment*) Chiselurs don't care a damn now about their parents. They're bringin' their fathers' grey hairs with sorra to the grave, an' laffin' at it, laffin' at it! (*He turns to* L *and sits down in the chair by the fire*) Ah, I suppose the same everywhere—the whole worl's in a state of chassis! Breakfast. Well, they can keep their breakfast for me. (*Emphatically*) Not if they went down on their bended knees, would I take it! I'll show them I've a little spirit left in me still. (*He sits still for a few moments; then gets up very slowly, crosses the stage behind the table, and goes to the dresser. He opens the bottom cupboard, takes out a plate and looks at it. Scornfully*) Sassige! Well, let her keep her sassige. (*He puts the plate of sausages back in the cupboard; returns slowly to the chair by the fire; sits down, and remains still for a few seconds; then he takes the teapot from the hob, and shakes it*) Uh, the tea's wet, right enough. (*He replaces the teapot on the hob, and again sits still for a few moments. Then he rises, crosses the stage slowly, behind the table, to the dresser, takes out the plate of sausages, returns to the fire, puts the sausages on the pan, puts both on the fire, sits down in the chair, and attends to the sausages with a fork*)

(*Singing as he cooks*) When the robins nest agen,
And the flowers are in bloom,
When the Springtime's sunny smile seems to banish all sorrow an' gloom;
Then me bonny blue-ey'd lad, if me heart be true till then—
He's promised he'll come back to me,
When the robins nest agen!
(*He lifts his head at the high note, and then drops his eyes to the pan*)
(*Singing*) When the . . .

(*Steps are heard approaching; he whips the pan off the fire and puts it under the bed, then sits down at the fire. The door opens and a bearded man looking in, says:* "You don't happen to want a sewin' machine?")

Boyle (*furiously*) No, I don't want e'er a sewin' machine! (*He returns the pan to the fire, and commences to sing again*)

(*Singing*) When the robins nest agen,
And the flowers are in bloom,
He's . . .

(*A thundering knock is heard at the street door*)

There's a terrible tatheraraa—that's a stranger—that's nobody belongin' to the house.

(*Another loud knock*)

JOXER (*sticking his head in at the door*) Did ye hear them tatherarahs?

BOYLE. Well, Joxer, I'm not deaf.

JOHNNY (*appearing in his shirt and trousers at the door on* L; *his face is anxious and his voice is tremulous*) Who's that at the door; who's that at the door? Who gave that knock—d'ye yous hear me—are yous deaf or dhrunk or what?

BOYLE (*to Johnny*) How the hell do I know who 'tis? Joxer, stick your head out o' the window an' see.

JOXER. An' mebbe get a bullet in the kisser? Ah, none o' them thricks for Joxer! It's betther to be a coward than a corpse!

(BOYLE *gets up from the chair, goes cautiously across the stage, behind the table to the window above the door* R. *He carefully shoves the curtains aside, and cautiously peeps out into the street*)

BOYLE. It's a fella in a thrench coat.

JOHNNY (*terrified*) Holy Mary, Mother of God! I——

BOYLE. He's goin' away—he must ha' got tired knockin'.

(JOHNNY *goes back to the room* L.

BOYLE *comes back to the fire, and attends to the sausages.* JOXER *remains standing beside the door* R. BOYLE *turns with a fork the sausage in the pan; turns round and gives an invitatory gesture to Joxer*)

Sit down an' have a cup o' tay, Joxer.

JOXER. I'm afraid the missus ud pop in on us agen before we'd know where we are. Somethin's tellin' me to go at wanst.

BOYLE. Don't be superstitious, man; we're Dublin men, an' not boyos that's only afther comin' up from the bog o' Allen —though if she did come in, right enough, we'd be caught like rats in a thrap.

JOXER. An' you know the sort she is—she wouldn't listen to reason—an' wanse bitten twice shy.

(BOYLE *thinks for a moment, leaves the pan on the hob, goes over to the window* C *back, lifts up and down the bottom part*)

BOYLE (*to Joxer*) If the worst came to the worst, you could dart out here, Joxer.

(JOXER *comes over to the window* C *back, and stands beside Boyle*)

It's only a dhrop of a few feet to the roof of the return room, an' the first minute she goes into the other room I'll give you the bend, an' you can slip in an' away.

JOXER (*yielding to temptation*) Ah, I won't stop very long, anyhow.

(JOXER *goes to the table, takes a chair, and sits down at the* R *end of the table.* BOYLE *goes back to the fire, and takes the pan in his hand again*)

(*Picking a book from the table*) Who's is the buk?

BOYLE. Aw, one o' Mary's; she's always readin' lately—nothin' but thrash, too. There's one I was lookin' at dh'other day: three stories, The Doll's House, Ghosts, an' The Wild Duck—buks only fit for chiselurs! (*He puts sausage on his own plate, and the gravy on Joxer's*)

JOXER. Didja ever rade *Elizabeth, or Th' Exile o' Sibayria* . . . ah, it's a darlin' story, a daarlin' story!

BOYLE. You eat your sassige, an' never min' *Th' Exile o' Sibayria.* (*He fills out tea, and sits down at the* L *end of the table*)

JOXER. What are you wearin' your moleskin trousers for?

BOYLE. I have to go to a job, Joxer. Just afther you'd gone, Devine kem runnin' in to tell us that Father Farrell said if I went down to the job that's goin' on in Rathmines I'd get a start.

JOXER (*congratulating Boyle*) Be the holy, that's good news!

BOYLE. How is it good news? I wondher if you were in my condition, would you call it good news?

JOXER (*dipping his bread in gravy*) I thought . . .

BOYLE. You thought! You think too sudden sometimes, Joxer. D'ye know, I'm hardly able to crawl with the pains in me legs!

JOXER. Yis, yis; I forgot the pains in your legs. I know you can do nothin' while they're at you.

BOYLE. You forgot; I don't think any of yous realize the state I'm in with the pains in me legs. What ud happen if I had to carry a bag o' cement?

JOXER. Ah, any man havin' the like of them pains id be down an' out, down an' out.

BOYLE. I wouldn't mind if he had said it to meself; but, no, oh no, he rushes in an' shouts it out in front o' Juno, an' you know what Juno is, Joxer. We all know Devine knows a little more than the rest of us, but he doesn't act as if he did; he's a good boy, sober, able to talk an' all that, but still . . .

JOXER. Oh ay; able to argufy, but still . . .

BOYLE. If he's runnin' afther Mary, aself, he's not goin' to be runnin' afther me. Captain Boyle's able to take care of himself. Afther all, I'm not gettin' brought up on Virol. I never heard him usin' a curse; I don't believe he was ever dhrunk in his life—sure he's not like a Christian at all!

JOXER. You're afther takin' the word out o' me mouth—afther all, a Christian's natural, but he's unnatural.

BOYLE. His oul' fella was just the same—a Wicklow man.

JOXER. A Wicklow man! That explains the whole thing. I've

met many a Wicklow man in me time, but I never met wan that was any good.

BOYLE. "Father Farrell," says he, "sent me down to tell you." Father Farrell! . . . D'ye know, Joxer, I never like to be beholden to any o' the clergy.

JOXER. It's dangerous, right enough.

BOYLE. If they do anything for you, they'd want you to be livin' in the Chapel. . . . (*With great solemnity*) I'm goin' to tell you somethin', Joxer, that I wouldn't tell to anybody else—the clergy always had too much power over the people in this unfortunate country.

JOXER. You could sing that if you had an air to it!

BOYLE (*becoming enthusiastic*) Didn't they prevent the people in "'forty-seven" from seizin' the corn, an' they starvin'; didn't they down Parnell; didn't they say that hell wasn't hot enough nor eternity long enough to punish the Fenians? We don't forget, we don't forget them things, Joxer. If they've taken everything else from us, Joxer, they've left us our memory.

JOXER (*lilting emotionally*) For mem'ry's the only friend that grief can call its own, that grief . . . can . . . call . . . its own!

BOYLE. Father Farrell's beginnin' to take a great intherest in Captain Boyle; because of what Johnny did for his country, says he to me wan day. It's a curious way to reward Johnny be makin' his poor oul' father work. But, that's what the clergy want, Joxer —work, work, work for me an' you; havin' us mulin' from mornin' till night, so that they may be in betther fettle when they come hoppin' round for their dues! Job! Well, let him give his job to wan of his hymn-singin', prayer-spoutin', craw-thumpin' Confraternity men!

(*The voice of a* COAL-BLOCK VENDOR *is heard chanting in the street*)

VOICE OF COAL VENDOR. Blocks . . . coal-blocks! Blocks . . . coal-blocks!

JOXER. God be with the young days when you were steppin' the deck of a manly ship, with the win' blowin' a hurricane through the masts, an' the only sound you'd hear was, "Port your helm!" an' the only answer, "Port it is, sir!"

BOYLE. Them was days, Joxer, them was days. Nothin' was too hot or too heavy for me then. Sailin' from the Gulf o' Mexico to the Antanartic Ocean. I seen things, I seen things, Joxer, that no mortal man should speak about that knows his Catechism. Ofen, an' ofen, when I was fixed to the wheel with a marlinspike, an' the win's blowin' fierce an' the waves lashin' an' lashin', till you'd think every minute was goin' to be your last, an' it blowed, an' blowed—blew is the right word, Joxer, but blowed is what the sailors use. . . .

JOXER. Aw, it's a darlin' word, a daarlin' word.

BOYLE. An', as it blowed an' blowed, I ofen looked up at the sky (*looks up at the ceiling*) an' assed meself the question—what is the stars, what is the stars?

VOICE OF COAL VENDOR. Any blocks, coal-blocks; blocks, coal-blocks!

JOXER. Ah, that's the question, that's the question—what is the stars?

BOYLE. An' then, I'd have another look, an' I'd ass meself (*looking at the ceiling*) what is the moon?

JOXER. Ah, that's the question (*looking at the ceiling*) what is the moon, what is the moon?

(*Rapid steps are heard coming towards the door* R. BOYLE *hastily starts to gather the breakfast things together.* JOXER *flies to the window, back* C. *The door* R *opens, and the black face of the* COAL-BLOCK VENDOR *peeps into the room*)

COAL-BLOCK VENDOR. D'ye yous want any blocks?

BOYLE (*with a roar of anger*) No, we don't want any blocks!

(BOYLE *has got a fright, and stands limply beside the fireplace.* JOXER *has got a fright, too, comes from the window, and stands* R *of Boyle*)

JOXER (*coming back with a sigh of relief*) That's afther puttin' the heart across me—I could ha' sworn it was Juno. I'd betther be goin', Captain; you couldn't tell the minute Juno'd hop in on us.

BOYLE. Let her hop in; we may as well have it out first as at last. I've made up me mind—I'm not goin' to do only what she damn well likes.

JOXER. Them sentiments does you credit, Captain; I don't like to say anything as between man an' wife, but I say as a butty, as a butty, Captain, that you've stuck it too long, an' that it's about time you showed a little spunk. How can a man die betther than facin' fearful odds, "For th' ashes of his fathers an' the temples of his gods."

BOYLE. She has her rights—there's no one denyin' it, but haven't I me rights too?

JOXER. Of course you have—the sacred rights o' man! (*He puts a hand on Boyle's shoulder*)

BOYLE. Today, Joxer, there's goin' to be issued a proclamation be me, establishin' an independent Republic, an' Juno'll have to take an oath of allegiance.

JOXER. Be firm, be firm, Captain; the first few minutes'll be the worst:—if you gently touch a nettle it'll sting you for your pains; grasp it like a lad of mettle, an' as soft as silk remains!

VOICE OF MRS BOYLE (*outside*) Can't stop, Mrs Madigan—I haven't a minute!

JOXER (*almost paralysed*) Holy God, here she is!

(JOXER, *in a terrible state of fear, rushes to the window back* C, *opens it and climbs hastily out on to the roof outside.* BOYLE *catches the ends of the tablecloth, leaving the things within, makes a huge bag of the cloth, runs over to the dresser back* R, *and crams the bundle into the bottom cupboard. He runs back to the fireplace, sits down on the chair, which he pulls from the table as he passes, and gazes quietly into the fire*)

BOYLE. I knew that fella ud stop till she was in on top of us!

(MRS BOYLE *enters hastily; she is flurried and excited*)

MRS BOYLE (*with a look of surprise at Boyle*) Oh, you're in—you must have been only afther comin' in?

BOYLE. No, I never went out.

MRS BOYLE. It's curious, then, you never heard the knockin'. (*She puts her coat and hat on the bed in the alcove*)

BOYLE. Knockin'? Of course I heard the knockin'.

MRS BOYLE. An' why didn't you open the door, then? I suppose you were so busy with Joxer that you hadn't time.

BOYLE. I haven't seen Joxer since I seen him before. Joxer! What ud bring Joxer here?

MRS BOYLE (*beginning to tidy the room, dust chairs, etc.*) D'ye mean to tell me that the pair of yous wasn't collogin' together here when me back was turned?

BOYLE. What ud we be collogin' together about? I have somethin' else to think of besides collogin' with Joxer. I can swear on all the holy prayer-books . . .

MRS BOYLE. That you weren't in no snug! (*She comes over to Boyle*) Go on in at wanst now, an' take off that moleskin trousers o' yours, an' put on a collar an' tie to smarten yourself up a bit. There's a visitor comin' with Mary in a minute, an' he has great news for you.

BOYLE (*standing up, protestingly*) A job, I suppose; let us get wan first before we start lookin' for another.

MRS BOYLE. That's the thing that's able to put the win' up you. Well, it's no job, but news that'll give you the chance o' your life.

BOYLE. What's all the mysthery about?

MRS BOYLE. G'win an take off the moleskin trousers when you're told!

(BOYLE *goes into the room on* L.

MRS BOYLE *tidies up the room, puts the shovel under the bed, and goes to the press*)

Oh, God bless us, looka the way everything's thrun about! Oh, Joxer was here, Joxer was here!

(MARY *enters with* CHARLIE BENTHAM; *he is a young man of twenty-five, tall, good-looking, with a very high opinion of himself generally. He is dressed in a brown coat, brown knee-breeches, grey stockings, a brown sweater, with a deep blue tie; he carries gloves and a walking-stick*)

(*Fussing round*) Come in, Mr Bentham; sit down, Mr Bentham, in this chair; it's more comfortabler than that, Mr Bentham. Himself'll be here in a minute; he's just takin' off his trousers.

MARY. Mother!

BENTHAM (*sitting in the chair back of the table,* R *end*) Please don't put yourself to any trouble, Mrs Boyle—I'm quite all right here, thank you.

MRS BOYLE. An' to think of you knowin' Mary, an' she knowin' the news you had for us, an' wouldn't let on; but it's all the more welcomer now, for we were on our last lap! (*She tidies things on the dresser*) You must excuse th' state o' th' place, Mr Bentham; th' minute I turn me back that man o' mine always makes a litther o' th' place, a litther o' th' place.

BENTHAM. Don't worry, Mrs Boyle; it's all right, I assure . . .

BOYLE (*inside the room* L) Where's me braces; where in th' name o' God did I leave me braces. . . . Ay, did you see where I put me braces?

JOHNNY (*inside, calling out*) Ma, will you come in here an' take da away ou' o' this or he'll dhrive me mad.

MRS BOYLE (*going towards the door*) Dear, dear, dear, that man'll be lookin' for somethin' on the day of judgement. (*She crosses over back to the door of the room* L *and calls in to Boyle*) Look at your braces, man, hanging round your neck.

BOYLE (*inside the room* L) Aw, holy God!

MRS BOYLE (*calling to Johnny, in the room* L) Johnny, Johnny, come out here for a minute.

JOHNNY (*replying from the room* L) Ah, leave Johnny alone, an' don't be annoyin' him!

MRS BOYLE. Come on, Johnny, till I inthroduce you to Mr Bentham. (*To Bentham*) Me son, Mr Bentham; he's afther goin' through the mill. He was only a chiselur of a Boy Scout in Easter Week, when he got hit in the hip; and his arm was blew off in the fight in O'Connell Street.

(JOHNNY *comes in*)

Here he is, Mr Bentham; Mr Bentham, Johnny. None can deny he done his bit for Irelan', if that's goin' to do him any good.

JOHNNY (*boastfully*) I'd do it agen, ma, I'd do it agen; for a principle's a principle.

MRS BOYLE. Ah, you lost your best principle, me boy, when you lost your arm; them's the only sort o' principles that's any good to a workin' man.

JOHNNY. Ireland only half free'll never be at peace while she has a son left to pull a trigger. (*He leaves Bentham, crosses to the fire, and sits down on the chair there*)

MRS BOYLE. To be sure, to be sure—no bread's a lot betther than half a loaf. (*She calls to Boyle in the room* L) Will you hurry up, there?

(BOYLE *comes in from the room* L. *He is wearing his best trousers, which aren't too good, and looks uncomfortable in a collar and tie.* MRS BOYLE *takes* BOYLE *by the arm, leads him to Bentham, and introduces them. They shake hands in an awkward way.* BOYLE *is to the* L, BENTHAM *to the* R, *and* MRS BOYLE *in* C)

This is me husband; Mr Boyle, Mr Bentham.

BENTHAM. Ah, very glad to know you, Mr Boyle. How are you?

BOYLE. Ah, I'm not too well at all; I suffer terrible with pains in me legs. Juno can tell you there what . . .

MRS BOYLE. You won't have many pains in your legs when you hear what Mr Bentham has to tell you.

BENTHAM. Juno! What an interesting name! It reminds one of Homer's glorious story of ancient gods and heroes.

BOYLE (*who doesn't know what he means*) Yis, doesn't it? You see, Juno was born an' christened in June; I met her in June; we were married in June, an' Johnny was born in June, so wan day I says to her, "You should ha' been called Juno," an' the name stuck to her ever since.

MRS BOYLE. Here, we can talk o' them things agen; let Mr Bentham say what he has to say now.

(MRS BOYLE *sets a chair for Bentham in front of the table,* R *end;* BOYLE *carries a chair to the front of the table,* L *end;* MRS BOYLE *sits down on the chair behind the table.* BENTHAM *and* BOYLE *sit down on their chairs, facing the audience.* JOHNNY *remains near the fire, but turns to hear what is to be said.* MARY *stands behind the chair of Boyle.* BENTHAM *takes a large-looking document from his breast pocket, opens it out. There is a feeling of suppressed excitement*)

BENTHAM (*pulling his chair a little closer to Boyle*) Well, Mr Boyle, I suppose you'll remember a Mr Ellison of Santry—he's a relative of yours, I think?

BOYLE (*viciously*) Is it that prognosticator an' procrastinator! Of course I remember him.

BENTHAM. Well, he's dead, Mr Boyle . . .

BOYLE. Sorra many'll go into mournin' for him.

MRS BOYLE. Wait till you hear what Mr Bentham has to say, an' then, maybe, you'll change your opinion.

BENTHAM. A week before he died he sent for me to write his will for him. He told me that there were two only that he wished to leave his property to: his second cousin, Michael Finnegan of Santry, and John Boyle his first cousin of Dublin.

BOYLE (*excitedly*) Me, is it me, me?

BENTHAM. You, Mr Boyle; I'll read a copy of the will that I

have here with me, which has been duly filed in the Court of Probate. (*He takes a paper from his pocket and reads*)

"6*th February*, 1922.

This is the last Will and Testament of William Ellison, of Santry, in the County of Dublin. I hereby order and wish my property to be sold and divided as follows:—

£20 to the St Vincent De Paul Society.

£60 for Masses for the repose of my soul (5*s.* for Each Mass).

The rest of my property to be divided between my first and second cousins.

I hereby appoint Timothy Buckly, of Santry, and Hugh Brierly, of Coolock, to be my Executors.

(*Signed*) WILLIAM ELLISON.
HUGH BRIERLY.
TIMOTHY BUCKLY.
CHARLES BENTHAM, N.T."

BOYLE (*eagerly*) An' how much'll be comin' out of it, Mr Bentham?

BENTHAM. The executors told me that half of the property would be anything between fifteen hundred and two thousand pounds.

MARY. A fortune, father, a fortune!

JOHNNY. We'll be able to get out o' this place now, an' go somewhere we're not known.

MRS BOYLE. You won't have to trouble about a job for awhile, Jack.

BOYLE (*fervently*) I'll never doubt the goodness o' God agen.

BENTHAM. I congratulate you, Mr Boyle.

(*They shake hands*)

BOYLE (*jumping up from the chair*) An' now, Mr Bentham, you'll have to have a wet.

BENTHAM (*puzzled*) A wet?

BOYLE. A wet—a jar—a boul!

MRS BOYLE (*horrified*) Jack, you're speakin' to Mr Bentham, an' not to Joxer.

BOYLE (*solemnly*) Juno . . . (*looking at Mary*) Mary . . . (*looking at Johnny*) Johnny . . . we'll have to go into mournin' at wanst . . . I never expected that poor Bill ud die so sudden . . . Well, we all have to die some day . . . you, Juno, today . . . an' me, maybe, tomorrow . . . It's sad, but it can't be helped . . . Requiescat in pace . . . or, usin' our oul' tongue like St Patrick or St Briget, Guh sayeree jeea ayera!

MARY (*laughing*) Oh, father, that's not Rest in Peace; that's God save Ireland.

BOYLE. U-u-ugh, it's all the same—isn't it a prayer? . . . Juno, I'm done with Joxer; he's nothin' but a prognosticator an' a . . .

(Suddenly the window in the wall, C *back, is violently pulled up, and* JOXER *angrily and rapidly climbs into the room. He runs to the door* R. *They are all startled at his entrance.* BENTHAM *retreats to back of the stage, round the* R *end of the table, and stands* L *of the dresser.* MARY *goes* L *of the table and stands on the* L *of* BENTHAM. BOYLE *retreats towards* L. MRS BOYLE *remains standing behind the table)*

JOXER *(turning at the door* R*)* You're done with Joxer, are you? Maybe you thought I'd stop on the roof all the night for you! Joxer out on the roof with the win' blowin' through him was nothin' to you an' your friend with the collar an' tie!

MRS BOYLE. What in the name o' God brought you out on the roof; what were you doin' there?

JOXER *(ironically)* I was dreamin' I was standin' on the bridge of a ship, an' she sailin' the Antharatic Ocean; an' it blowed, an' blowed, an' me lookin' up at the sky, an' sayin', "what is the stars, what is the stars?"

(MRS BOYLE *leaves the back of the table, hurries down to the door* R *in a determined manner, opens the door, angrily, and stands beside it)*

MRS BOYLE. Here, get ou' o' this, Joxer Daly; I was always thinkin' you had a slate off.

JOXER *(moving to the door)* I have to laugh every time I look at the deep-sea sailor; an' a row on a river ud' make him sea-sick!

BOYLE. Get ou' o' this before I take the law into me own hands!

JOXER *(going out)* Say aw rewaeawr, but not good-bye. Lookin' for work, an' prayin' to God he won't get it!

(JOXER *goes)*

MRS BOYLE. I'm tired tellin' you what Joxer was; maybe now you see yourself the kind he is.

BOYLE *(fervently)* He'll never blow the froth off a pint o' mine agen, that's a sure thing. Johnny . . . Mary . . . you're to keep yourselves to yourselves for the future. Juno, I'm done with Joxer. . . . I'm a new man from this out . . .

(BOYLE *moves to* R. MRS BOYLE *comes* L. *They meet* C, *clasp hands and sing emotionally:)*

Oh, me darlin' Juno, I will be thrue to thee.
Me own, me darlin' Juno, you're all the world to me.

CURTAIN

ACT II

SCENE—*The same room, but the furniture is richer looking.*

A highly polished chest of drawers stands where the dresser was, L *back. The window, back* L *of the chest of drawers, is curtained with a gaudy-patterned cretonne. The table is covered with a dark red embroidered cloth. Down stage* R *is a gaudily upholstered sofa, three chairs upholstered in the same way, one at each end of the table and one by the fire. A large vase, filled with gay artificial flowers, is on top of the chest of drawers,* R *end. At the other end are a cheap tea-set, a bottle of whisky and several bottles of stout. A lamp, with a silken shade, is lighted on the table. There are a few cheap pictures on the walls. Coloured Christmas paper-chains hang from the four corners of the ceiling, meeting in the* C. *The votive light, under the picture of the Blessed Virgin, is still burning.*

BOYLE, *in his shirt-sleeves, is voluptuously stretched on the sofa, smoking a pipe. He is half-asleep. After a few moments' pause the voice of* JOXER, *outside the door* R, *is heard lilting softly:* "Me pipe I'll smoke, as I drive me moke,—are you there, mor . . . ee . . . ar . . . i . . . teee?"

BOYLE *rises at once to a sitting posture; takes a small attaché-case from under the sofa, opens it, takes out writing-paper; takes a fountain-pen from his breast pocket, and pretends to be busy writing. He puts the case on his knees and uses it as a desk.*

BOYLE (*calling out*) Come along, Joxer, me son; come along.

JOXER (*putting his head in at the door* R) Are you be yourself?

BOYLE. Come on, come on; that doesn't matther; I'm masther now, an' I'm goin' to remain masther.

(JOXER *comes in at the door* R)

JOXER. How d'ye feel now, as a man o' money?

BOYLE (*solemnly*) It's a responsibility, Joxer, a great responsibility.

JOXER. I suppose 'tis now, though you wouldn't think it.

BOYLE. Ever since the Will was passed I've run hundhreds o' dockyments through me han's—I tell you, you have to keep your wits about you. (*He busies himself with papers*)

JOXER (*about to go*) Well, I won't disturb you; I'll dhrop in when . . .

BOYLE (*hastily*) It's all right, Joxer, this is the last one to be signed today. (*He signs a paper, puts it into the attaché-case, which he shuts with a snap. He screws on the cap of the fountain-pen, puts it back in his breast pocket, and sits back with an important air on the sofa*) Now, Joxer, you want to see me? I'm at your service. What can I do for you, me man?

JOXER. I've just dhropped in with the three pound five that Mrs Madigan riz on the blankets an' table for you, an' she says you're to be in no hurry payin' it back. (*He takes the money out of his pocket and gives it to Boyle*)

BOYLE. She won't be long without it; I expect the first cheque for a couple o' hundhred any day. There's the five bob for yourself—(*offers him the money*) go on, take it, man; it'll not be the last you'll get from the Captain. Now an' agen we have our differ, but we're together all the time.

JOXER (*pocketing the money given by Boyle*) Me for you, an' you for me, like the two Musketeers.

BOYLE. Father Farrell stopped me today an' tole me how glad he was I fell in for the money.

JOXER (*sitting down at the* R *end of the sofa*) He'll be stoppin' you ofen enough now; I suppose it was "Mr" Boyle with him?

BOYLE. He shuk me be the han'. . . .

JOXER (*ironically*) I met with Napper Tandy, an' he shuk me be the han'!

BOYLE (*admonishingly*) You're seldom asthray, Joxer, but you're wrong shipped this time. What you're sayin' of Father Farrell is very near to blasfeemey. I don't like anyone to talk disrespectful of Father Farrell.

JOXER. You're takin' me up wrong, Captain; I wouldn't let a word be said agen Father Farrell—the heart o' the rowl, that's what he is; I always said he was a darlin' man, a daarlin' man.

BOYLE. Comin' up the stairs who did I meet but that bummer, Nugent. "I seen you talkin' to Father Farrell," says he, with a grin on him. "He'll be folleyin' you," says he, "like a Guardian Angel from this out"—all the time the oul' grin on him, Joxer.

JOXER. I never seen him yet but he had that oul' grin on him!

BOYLE (*with dignity*) "Mr Nugent," says I, "Father Farrell is a man o' the people, an', as far as I know the History o' me country, the priests was always in the van of the fight for Irelan's freedom."

JOXER (*fervently*) "Who was it led the van, Soggart Aroon?
Since the fight first began, Soggart Aroon?"

BOYLE. "Who are you tellin'?" says he. "Didn't they let down the Fenians, an' didn't they do in Parnell? An' now . . ." "You ought to be ashamed o' yourself," says I, interruptin' him, "not to know the History o' your country." An' I left him gawkin', where he was.

JOXER. Where ignorance's bliss 'tis folly to be wise; I wondher did he ever read the Story o' Irelan'.

BOYLE. Be J. L. Sullivan? Don't you know he didn't.

JOXER (*rubbing his hands*) Ah, it's a darlin' buk, a daarlin' buk!

BOYLE. You'd betther be goin' now, Joxer, his Majesty, Bentham, 'll be here any minute, now.

JOXER. Be the way things is lookin', it'll be a match between him an' Mary. She's thrun over Jerry altogether. Well, I hope it will, for he's a darlin' man.

BOYLE. I'm glad you think so—I don't. (*Irritably*) What's darlin' about him?

JOXER (*nonplussed*) I only seen him twiced, if you want to know me, come an' live with me.

BOYLE (*scornfully*) He's too ignified for me—to hear him talk you'd think he knew as much as a Boney's Oraculum. He's given up his job as teacher, an' is goin' to become a solicitor in Dublin—he's been studyin' law. I suppose he thinks I'll set him up, but he's wrong shipped. An' th' other fella—Jerry's as bad. The two o' them ud give you a pain in your face, listenin' to them; Jerry believin' in nothin', an' Bentham believin' in everythin'. One that says all is God an' no man; an' th' other that says all is man an' no God!

JOXER (*getting up*) Well, I'll be off now.

BOYLE (*getting up off the sofa*) Don't forget to dhrop down afther awhile; we'll have a quiet jar, an' a song or two.

JOXER (*going towards the door* R) Never fear.

BOYLE (*following Joxer*) An' tell Mrs Madigan that I hope we'll have the pleasure of her organization at our little enthertainment.

JOXER. Righto; we'll come down together.

(JOXER *goes out by the door* R.

BOYLE *shuts the door* R, *after Joxer, as* JOHNNY *comes out from the room,* L, *goes to the fire, and sits down moodily on a chair there.* BOYLE, *filling his pipe, looks at him for a few moments, and shakes his head, as much as to say, there goes a hopeless case. He is crossing back to the sofa, when* MRS BOYLE'S *voice is heard speaking outside the door* R)

MRS BOYLE'S VOICE (*outside the door* R) Open the door, Jack—this thing has me nearly killed with the weight.

(BOYLE *turns, runs to the door* R, *and opens it.*

MRS BOYLE *enters carrying a gramophone, followed by* MARY *carrying a gramophone horn and a few parcels.* MRS BOYLE *leaves the gramophone on top of the chest of drawers, takes the horn from Mary and fixes it in the gramophone.* MARY *leaves the parcels, containing cakes, on the table*)

MRS BOYLE (*out of breath*) Carrying that from Henry Street was no joke.

(BOYLE *stands back and gazes at the gramophone in admiration. All except Johnny look at the instrument*)

BOYLE (*admiringly*) Uh, that's a grand-looking insthrument! How much was it?

(MRS BOYLE *takes off her hat and coat, leaving them in the alcove, back*)

MRS BOYLE. Pound down, an' five to be paid at two shillin's a week.

BOYLE. That's reasonable enough.

MRS BOYLE. I'm afraid we're runnin' into too much debt; first the furniture, an' now this.

BOYLE (*dismissing an anxiety*) The whole lot won't be much out of two thousand pounds.

MARY (*at the window,* C *back*) I don't know what you wanted a gramophone for—I know Charlie hates them; he says they're destructive of real music.

BOYLE (*indignantly*) Desthructive of music—that fella ud give you a pain in your face. All a gramophone wants is to be properly played; its thrue wondher is only felt when everythin's quiet—what a gramophone wants is dead silence!

MARY. But, father, Jerry says the same; afther all you can only appreciate music when your ear is properly trained.

BOYLE. That's another fella ud give you a pain in your face. Properly thrained! I suppose you couldn't appreciate football unless your fut was properly thrained.

MRS BOYLE (*to Mary*) Go on in ower that an' dress, or Charlie 'll be in on you, an' tea nor nothin'll be ready.

(MARY *goes into the room* L.

MRS BOYLE *opens the parcels, takes the cakes out and puts them on the plate taken from the chest of drawers. She goes on arranging things for tea on the table*)

(*Looking over anxiously at Johnny*) You didn't look at our new gramophone, Johnny?

JOHNNY. 'Tisn't gramophones I'm thinking of.

MRS BOYLE. An' what is it you're thinkin' of, allanna?

JOHNNY. Nothin', nothin', nothin'.

MRS BOYLE. Sure, you must be thinkin' of somethin'; it's yourself that has yourself the way y'are; sleepin' wan night in me sisther's, an' the nex' in your father's brother's—you'll get no rest goin' on that way.

JOHNNY. I can rest nowhere, nowhere, nowhere.

MRS BOYLE. Sure, you're not thryin' to rest anywhere.

JOHNNY. Let me alone, let me alone, let me alone, for God's sake.

(*There is a knock at the street door*)

MRS BOYLE (*in a flutter*) Here he is; here's Mr Bentham!

BOYLE. Well, there's room for him; it's a pity there's not a brass band to play him in.

MRS BOYLE. We'll han' the tea round, an' not be clusthered round the table, as if we never seen nothin'.

(*There is another knock at the door* R. MRS BOYLE *goes to it excitedly, opens it, and* BENTHAM *comes in*)

(*To Bentham, effusively*) Give your hat and stick to Jack, there . . .

(BENTHAM *crosses the stage in front of the table to Boyle,* L, *and offers his hat and stick.* BOYLE, *with a sour grimace, takes them reluctantly, goes up stage between the table and the sofa, and throws them contemptuously in the corner above the door* L. MRS BOYLE *places a chair* L *below the fireplace*)

Sit down, Mr Bentham, in this chair by the fire. Mary'll be out to you in a minute.

(BENTHAM *sits on the chair given by* MRS BOYLE. BOYLE *comes down stage, gets a chair, and sits down above the fireplace, almost facing Bentham, but in full view of the audience.* MRS BOYLE *goes back behind the table to the dresser, and continues to arrange for tea*)

BOYLE (*solemnly and with an air of great importance*) I seen be the paper this mornin' that Consols was down half per cent. That's serious, min' you, an' shows the whole counthry's in a state o' chassis.

MRS BOYLE. What's Consols, Jack?

BOYLE. Consols? Oh, Consols is—oh, there's no use tellin' women what Consols is—th' wouldn't undherstand.

BENTHAM. It's just as you were saying, Mr Boyle . . .

(MARY *comes in, charmingly dressed, from the room* L; *she comes down to the* L *end of the table, and stands facing Bentham.* BENTHAM *rises, shakes hands with* MARY, *and sits down again.* MARY *is wearing a blue ribbon fillet round her hair, and has a green one in her hand*)

Oh, good evening, Mary; how pretty you're looking!

MARY (*archly*) Am I?

BOYLE. We were just talkin' when you kem in, Mary; I was tellin' Mr Bentham that the whole counthry's in a state o' chassis.

MARY (*to Bentham*) Would you prefer the green or the blue ribbon round me hair, Charlie?

MRS BOYLE (*expostulating*) Mary, your father's speakin'.

BOYLE (*rapidly*) I was jus' tellin' Mr Bentham that the whole counthry's in a state o' chassis.

MARY. I'm sure you're frettin', da, whether it is or no.

MRS BOYLE. With all our churches an' religions, the worl's not a bit the betther.

BOYLE (*with a commanding gesture*) Tay!

(MARY *and* MRS BOYLE *serve the tea.* MRS BOYLE *pours tea into cups, and* MARY *carries them round, first to Bentham and then to Boyle, and last to Johnny*)

MRS BOYLE. An' Irelan's takin' a leaf out o' the worl's buk;

when we got the makin' of our own laws I thought we'd never stop to look behind us, but instead of that we never stopped to look before us! If the people ud folley up their religion betther there'd be a betther chance for us—what do you think, Mr Bentham?

BENTHAM. I'm afraid I can't venture to express an opinion on that point, Mrs Boyle; dogma has no attraction for me.

MRS BOYLE (*sitting drinking her tea behind the table*) I forgot you didn't hold with us: what's this you said you were?

BENTHAM. A Theosophist, Mrs Boyle.

MRS BOYLE. An' what in the name o' God's a Theosophist?

BOYLE. A Theosophist, Juno, 's a—tell her, Mr Bentham, tell her.

BENTHAM. It's hard to explain in a few words: Theosophy's founded on The Vedas, the religious books of the East. Its central theme is the existence of an all-pervading Spirit—the Life-Breath. Nothing really exists but this one Universal Life-Breath. And whatever even seems to exist separately from this Life-Breath, doesn't really exist at all. It is all vital force in man, in all animals, and in all vegetation. This Life-Breath is called the Prawna.

MRS BOYLE. The Prawna! What a comical name!

BOYLE. Prawna; yis, the Prawna. (*He blows gently through his lips*) That's the Prawna!

MRS BOYLE. Whist, whist, Jack.

BENTHAM (*leaving his cup and saucer back on the table*) The happiness of man depends upon his sympathy with this Spirit. Men who have reached a high state of excellence are called Yogi. Some men become Yogi in a short time, it may take others millions of years.

BOYLE. Yogi! I have seen hundhreds of them in the streets o' San Francisco.

BENTHAM. It is said by these Yogi that if we practise certain mental exercises that we would have powers denied to others—for instance, the faculty of seeing things that happen miles and miles away.

MRS BOYLE. I wouldn't care to meddle with that sort o' belief; it's a very curious religion, altogether.

BOYLE (*scornfully to Mrs Boyle. He leaves his cup and saucer back on the table*) What's curious about it? Isn't all religions curious; if they weren't, you wouldn't get anyone to believe them. But religions is passin' away—they've had their day like everything else. Take the real Dublin people, f'rinstance: they know more about Charlie Chaplin an' Tommy Mix than they do about Ess. Ess. Peter an' Paul!

MRS BOYLE. You don't believe in ghosts, Mr Bentham?

MARY. Don't you know he doesn't, mother?

BENTHAM. I don't know that, Mary. Scientists are beginning

to think that what we call ghosts are sometimes seen by persons of a certain nature. They say that sensational actions, such as the killing of a person, demands great energy, and that that energy lingers in the place where the action occurred. People may live in the place and see nothing, when someone may come along whose personality has some peculiar connexion with the energy of the place, and, in a flash, the person sees the whole affair.

Johnny (*rising swiftly from his seat by the fire, pale and trembling*) What sort of talk is this to be goin' on with? Is there nothin' betther to be talkin' about but the killin' of people? My God, isn't it bad enough for these things to happen without talkin' about them?

(Johnny *goes hurriedly into the room* l. Bentham *rises from his chair, surprised and agitated*)

Bentham. Oh, I'm very sorry, Mrs Boyle; I never thought . . .

Mrs Boyle (*apologetically*) Never mind, Mr Bentham; he's very touchy.

(*A frightened scream is heard from* Johnny *in the room* l. *They all rise from their chairs, startled*)

Mother of God, what's that?

(Johnny *rushes from the room* l, *his face pale, his lips twitching, and his limbs trembling.* Mrs Boyle *runs over and catches him in her arms*)

Johnny. Shut the door, shut the door, quick, for God's sake! Great God, have mercy on me. Blessed Mother o' God, shelther me, shelther your son!

Mrs Boyle. What's wrong with you—what ails you?

(Mrs Boyle *half-carries him to the bed in the alcove and puts him sitting there*)

Sit down, sit down, here on the bed . . . there now, there now.

Mary (*back of the table*) What ails you, Johnny?

Johnny. I seen him. I seen him . . . kneelin' in front of the statue . . . merciful Jesus, have pity on me!

Mrs Boyle (*sharply to Boyle*) Get him a little whisky . . . quick, man, an' don't stand gawkin'.

(Boyle *crosses to the chest of drawers* r *back, pours a little whisky into a glass, adds water, brings it to Mrs Boyle, and gives it to her.* Mrs Boyle *gives a drink to Johnny, returns the glass to* Boyle, *who goes back with the glass to the chest of drawers, leaves it down, and stands watching Johnny and Mrs Boyle*)

Johnny. Sit here, sit here, mother . . . between me an' the door.

Mrs Boyle (*comforting him*) I'll sit beside you as long as you like, only tell me what was it came across you at all?

JOHNNY. I seen him . . . I seen Robbie Tancred kneelin' down before the statue . . . an' the red light shinin' on him . . . an' when I went in . . . he turned an' looked at me . . . an' I seen the woun's bleedin' in his breast . . . Oh, why did he look at me like that . . . it wasn't my fault that he was done in . . . Mother o' God, keep him away from me!

MRS BOYLE (*soothingly*) There, there, child, you've imagined it all. There was nothin' there at all—it was the red light you seen, an' the talk we had put all the rest into your head. Here, dhrink more o' this—it'll do you good . . . An', now, stretch yourself down on the bed for a little. (*To Boyle*) Go in, Jack, an' show him it was only in his own head it was.

BOYLE (*making no move*) E-e-e-e-eh; it's all nonsense; it was only a shadda he saw.

MARY. Mother o' God, he made me heart lep!

BENTHAM. It was simply due to an overwrought imagination—we all get that way at times. (*He sits down again*)

MRS BOYLE. There, dear, lie down in the bed, an' I'll put the quilt across you . . . e-e-e-eh, that's it . . . (*She settles him lying on the bed*) you'll be as right as the mail in a few minutes.

JOHNNY. Mother, go into the room an' see if the light's lightin' before the statue.

MRS BOYLE (*to Boyle*) Jack, run in an' see if the light's lightin' before the statue.

BOYLE (*to Mary*) Mary, slip in an' see if the light's lightin' before the statue.

(MARY *hesitates to go in*)

BENTHAM. It's all right; Mary, I'll go. (*He goes into the room* L, *remains for a few moments, and returns*) Everything's just as it was—the light burning bravely before the statue.

BOYLE. Of course; I knew it was all nonsense.

(*There is a knock at the door* R)

(*Going to open the door*) E-e-e-e-eh.

(BOYLE *opens it, and* JOXER, *followed by* MRS MADIGAN, *enters.*
MRS MADIGAN *is a strong, dapper little woman of about forty-five; her face is almost always a widespread smile of complacency. She is a woman who, in manner at least, can mourn with them that mourn, and rejoice with them that do rejoice. When she is feeling comfortable, she is inclined to be reminiscent; when others say anything, or following a statement made by herself, she has a habit of putting her head a little to one side, and nodding it rapidly several times in succession, like a bird pecking at a hard berry. Indeed, she has a good deal of the bird in her, but the bird instinct is by no means a melodious one. She is ignorant, vulgar and forward, but her heart is generous withal. For instance, she would help a neighbour's sick child; she would probably kill the child,*

but her intentions would be to cure it; she would be more at home helping a drayman to lift a fallen horse. She is dressed in a rather soiled grey dress and a vivid purple blouse; in her hair is a huge comb, ornamented with huge coloured beads. She enters with a gliding step, beaming smile and nodding head. BOYLE *receives them effusively)*

BOYLE. Come on in, Mrs Madigan; come on in; I was afraid you weren't comin' . . . (*Slyly*) There's some people able to dhress, ay, Joxer?

JOXER. Fair as the blossoms that bloom in the May, an' sweet as the scent of the new-mown hay . . . Ah, well, she may wear them.

MRS MADIGAN (*looking at Mary*) I know some as are as sweet as the blossoms that bloom in the May—oh, no names, no pack dhrill!

BOYLE. An', now, I'll inthroduce the pair o' yous to Mary's intended: Mr Bentham, this is Mrs Madigan, an oul' back-parlour neighbour, that, if she could help it at all, ud never see a body shuk!

BENTHAM (*rising, and tentatively shaking the hand of Mrs Madigan*) I'm sure, it's a great pleasure to know you, Mrs Madigan.

MRS MADIGAN. An' I'm goin' to tell you, Mr Bentham, you're goin' to get as nice a bit o' skirt in Mary, there, as ever you seen in your puff. Not like some of the dhressed-up dolls that's knockin' about lookin' for men when it's a skelpin' they want. I remember, as well as I remember yestherday, the day she was born—of a Tuesday, the Twenty-fifth o' June, in the year nineteen-o-one, at thirty-three minutes past wan in the day be Foley's clock, the pub at the corner o' the street. A cowld day it was too, for the season o' the year, an' I remember sayin' to Joxer, there, who I met comin' up th' stairs, that the new arrival in Boyle's ud grow up a hardy chiselur if it lived, an' that she'd be somethin' one o' these days that nobody suspected, an' so signs on it, here she is today, goin' to be married to a young man lookin' as if he'd be fit to commensurate in any position in life it ud please God to call him!

BOYLE (*effusively, indicating the sofa to Mrs Madigan*) Sit down, sit down, Mrs Madigan, me oul' sport.

(MRS MADIGAN *sits down on the* R *end of the sofa.* BOYLE *turns round to* JOXER, *who is standing on his* R, *and guides him with an air of importance to be introduced to* BENTHAM, *who evidently doesn't like the look of Joxer)*

(*Effusively, to Bentham*) This is Joxer Daly, Past Chief Ranger of the Dear Little Shamrock Branch of the Irish National Foresters, an oul' front top neighbour who never despaired, even in the darkest days of Ireland's sorra.

(JOXER *vigorously shakes the hand of* BENTHAM, *who does not respond to the friendly feeling of Joxer)*

JOXER (*turning his head to Boyle*) Nil desperandum, nil desperandum, Captain.

BOYLE. Sit down, Joxer, sit down.

(BOYLE *indicates the chair at the* L *end of the table, and* JOXER *sits on it.* BOYLE *returns to the chest of drawers, back* R, *where the drink is. He gets a bottle of stout, brings it to the table and places it at Joxer's elbow, then goes back*)

(*Going to the chest of drawers*) The two of us was ofen in a tight corner.

MRS BOYLE. Ay, in Foley's snug!

JOXER. An' we kem out of it flyin', we kem out of it flyin', Captain.

BOYLE. An', now, for a dhrink—I know yous won't refuse an oul' friend.

MRS MADIGAN (*to Mrs Boyle*) Is Johnny not well, Mrs . . .

MRS BOYLE (*warningly*) S-s-s-sh.

MRS MADIGAN. Oh, the poor darlin'.

BOYLE. Well, Mrs Madigan, is it tea or what?

MRS MADIGAN. Well, speakin' for meself, I jus' had me tea a minute ago, an' I'm afraid to dhrink any more—I'm never the same when I dhrink too much tay. Thanks, all the same, Mr Boyle.

BOYLE. Well, what about a bottle o' stout or a dhrop o' whisky?

MRS MADIGAN. A bottle o' stout ud be a little too heavy for me stummock afther me tay . . . A-a-ah, I'll thry the ball o' malt.

(BOYLE, *at the chest of drawers, fills out whisky in a glass, and brings it with a small jug of water to Mrs Madigan. He gives the glass of whisky to Mrs Madigan and waits to put the water in*)

There's nothin' like a ball o' malt occasional like—too much of it isn't good. (*To* BOYLE, *who is adding water*) Ah, God, Johnny, don't put too much wather on it! (*She drinks*) I suppose yous'll be lavin' this place.

BOYLE. I'm looking for a place near the sea; I'd like the place that you might say was me cradle, to be me grave as well. The sea is always callin' me.

JOXER. She is callin', callin', callin', in the win' an' on the sea.

BOYLE. Another dhrop o' whisky, Mrs Madigan?

MRS MADIGAN. Well, now, it ud be hard to refuse seein' the suspicious times that's in it.

(*The party has settled down for a drink and a few songs. The positions are:* MRS BOYLE *sits at the* R *end of the table;* BOYLE, *back of the table;* JOXER, L *end of the table;* MRS MADIGAN, *to Joxer's* L, *on the* R *end of the sofa;* MARY *sits on the sofa,* L *of Mrs Madigan.* JOHNNY *on the bed in the alcove, lying down, resting on his elbow;*

BENTHAM *at the back*, L *of the alcove, looking on, not very interested in the proceedings*)

BOYLE (*rapping on the table authoritatively*) Song! Juno . . . Mary . . . home to our Mountains.

MRS MADIGAN (*enthusiastically*) Hear, hear.

(JOXER *takes the bottle of stout Boyle has left on the table for him, opens it, pours the beer into a glass, and takes a drink*)

JOXER (*delighted*) Oh, tha's a darlin' song, a daarlin' song!

MARY (*bashfully*) Ah no, da; I'm not in a singin' humour.

MRS MADIGAN. Gawn with you, child, an' you only goin' to be marrid; I remember as well as I remember yestherday—it was on a lovely August evenin', exactly, accordin' to date, fifteen years ago, come the Tuesday folleyin' the nex' that's comin' on, when me own man (the Lord be good to him) an' me was sittin' shy together in a doty little nook on a counthry road, adjacent to The Stiles. "That'll scratch your lovely, little white neck," says he, ketchin' hould of a danglin' bramble branch, holdin' clusters of the loveliest flowers you ever seen, an' breakin' it off, so that his arm fell, accidental like, roun' me waist, an' as I felt it tightenin' an' tightenin', an' tightenin', I thought me buzzum was every minute goin' to burst out into a roystherin' song about: The little green leaves that were shakin' on the threes, The gallivantin' butther-flies, an' buzzin' o' the bees!

BOYLE (*loudly rapping on the table*) Ordher, ordher for the song.

(MRS BOYLE *gets up from her chair and stands a little down stage*, R)

MRS BOYLE (*beckoning to Mary*) Come on, Mary, we'll do our best.

(MARY *crosses to* R *in front of the table, and stands on Mrs Boyle's left. They sing "Home to our Mountains". They sing the song simply. When the song is ended, they bow to the company, and return to their places, amid applause*, MRS BOYLE *to her chair, and* MARY *to the sofa*)

BOYLE (*emotionally, at the end of the song*) Lull . . . me . . . to . . . rest!

JOXER (*clapping his hands*) Bravo, bravo! Darlin' girulls, darlin' girulls!

MRS MADIGAN. Juno, I never seen you in betther form.

BENTHAM. Very nicely rendered indeed.

MRS MADIGAN. A noble call, a noble call!

MRS BOYLE. What about yourself, Mrs Madigan?

(*After some coaxing*, MRS MADIGAN *rises, and in a quavering voice sings the first verse of "The Young May Moon"*)

The young May moon is beaming, love,
The glow-worm's lamp is gleaming, love;
How sweet to rove
Through Morna's grove,
When the drowsy world is dreaming, love.
Then awake! The heavens look bright, my dear,
'Tis never too late for delight, my dear,
And the best of all ways
To lengthen our days
Is to steal a few hours from the night, my dear.

(*Becoming husky, amid applause, she sits down*) Ah, me voice is too husky, now, Juno, though I remember the time when Maisie Madigan could sing like a nightingale at matin' time. I remember as well as I remember yestherday, at a party given to celebrate the comin' of the first chiselur to Annie an' Benny Jimeson—who was the barber, yous may remember, in Henrietta Street, that, afther Easter Week, hung out a green, white an' orange pole, an', then, when the Tans started their Jazz dancin', whipped it in agen, an' stuck out a red, white an' blue wan instead, givin' as an excuse that a barber's pole was strictly non-political—singin' "An You'll Remember Me", with the top notes quiverin' in a dead hush of pethrified attention, folleyed be a clappin' o' han's that shuk the tumblers on the table, an' capped be Jimeson, the barber, sayin' that it was the best rendherin' of "You'll Remember Me" he ever heard in his natural!

BOYLE (*peremptorily*) Ordher for Joxer's song!

JOXER. Ah no, I couldn't; don't ass me, Captain.

BOYLE. Joxer's song, Joxer's song—give us wan of your shut-eyed wans.

(JOXER *settles himself in his chair; takes a drink; clears his throat; solemnly closes his eyes, and begins to sing in a very querulous voice*)

She is far from the lan' where her young hero sleeps,
An' lovers around her are sighing (*He hesitates*)
An' lovers around her are sighin' . . . sighin' . . . sighin' . . .

(*A pause*)

BOYLE (*imitating Joxer*) "And lovers around her are sighing!" What's the use of you thryin' to sing the song if you don't know it?

MARY. Thry another one, Mr Daly—maybe you'd be more fortunate.

MRS MADIGAN. Gawn, Joxer; thry another wan.

JOXER (*starting again*) I have heard the mavis singin' his love song to the morn;
I have seen the dew-dhrop clinging to the rose jus' newly born; but . . . but . . . (*frantically*) To the rose jus' newly born . . . newly born . . . born.

JOHNNY. Mother, put on the gramophone, for God's sake, an' stop Joxer's bawlin'.

BOYLE (*commandingly*) Gramophone! . . . I hate to see fellas thryin' to do what they're not able to do.

(BOYLE *arranges the gramophone, and is about to start it, when voices are heard of persons descending the stairs*)

MRS BOYLE (*warningly*) Whisht, Jack, don't put it on, don't put it on yet; this must be poor Mrs Tancred comin' down to go to the hospital—I forgot all about them bringin' the body to the church tonight.

(*The voices of* FIRST NEIGHBOUR *and* MRS TANCRED *are heard speaking outside the door* R)

FIRST NEIGHBOUR. It's a sad journey we're goin' on, but God's good, an' the Republicans won't be always down.

MRS TANCRED. Ah, what good is that to me now! Whether they're up or down, it won't bring me darlin' boy from the grave.

MRS BOYLE (*to Mary*) Open the door, Mary, an' give them a bit of light.

(MARY *crosses to* R *front of the table, and opens the door* R.

MRS TANCRED—*a very old woman—appears; she is obviously shaken by her son's death. She is accompanied by several neighbours.*

MRS BOYLE *runs to the door* R, *and sympathetically brings* MRS TANCRED *into the room.*

The neighbours are nearest the door R. FIRST NEIGHBOUR *on Mrs Tancred's* R, MRS BOYLE *stands on her* L; MARY *a little behind Mrs Boyle. The rest remain in their places*)

Come in an' have a hot cup o' tay, Mrs Tancred, before you go.

MRS TANCRED. Ah, I can take nothin' now, Mrs Boyle—I won't be long afther him.

FIRST NEIGHBOUR. Still an' all, he died a noble death, an' we'll bury him like a king.

MRS TANCRED. An' I'll go on livin' like a pauper. Ah, what's the pains I suffered bringin' him into the world to carry him to his cradle, to the pains I'm sufferin' now, carryin' him out o' the world to bring him to his grave!

MARY. It would be better for you not to go at all, Mrs Tancred, but to stay at home beside the fire with some o' the neighbours.

MRS TANCRED. I seen the first of him, an' I'll see the last of him.

MRS BOYLE. You'd want a shawl, Mrs Tancred; it's a cowld night, an' the win's blowin' sharp.

MRS MADIGAN (*crossing front and running out of the door* R) I've a shawl above.

MRS TANCRED. Me home is gone, now; he was me only child,

an' to think that he was lyin' for a whole night stretched out on the side of a lonely country lane, with his head, his darlin' head, that I ofen kissed an' fondled, half-hidden in the wather of a runnin' brook. An' I'm told he was the leadher of the ambush where me nex'-door neighbour, Mrs Mannin', lost her Free State soldier son. An' now here's the two of us oul' women, standin' one on each side of a scales o' sorra, balanced be the bodies of our two dead darlin' sons.

(MRS MADIGAN *returns, and wraps a shawl around her and returns to her seat on the sofa*)

God bless you, Mrs Madigan . . . (*She moves slowly towards the door*) Mother o' God, Mother o' God, have pity on the pair of us! . . . O Blessed Virgin, where were you when me darlin' son was riddled with bullets, when me darlin' son was riddled with bullets! . . . Sacred Heart of the Crucified Jesus, take away our hearts o' stone . . . an' give us hearts o' flesh! . . . Take away this murdherin' hate . . . an' give us Thine own eternal love!

(MRS TANCRED *and the neighbours go out by the door* R.

MARY *crosses over the stage, behind the table, to Bentham,* L *of the alcove, stops to say something to him (which isn't heard), then goes into the room* L.

MRS BOYLE *sits down on the chair* R *end of the table*)

MRS BOYLE (*explanatorily to Bentham*) That was Mrs Tancred of the two-pair back; her son was found, e'er yestherday, lyin' out beyant Finglas riddled with bullets. A Die-hard he was, be all accounts. He was a nice quiet boy, but lattherly he went to hell with his Republic first, an' Republic last an' Republic over all. He ofen took tea with us here, in the oul' days, an' Johnny, there, an' him used to be always together.

JOHNNY. Am I always to be havin' to tell you that he was no friend o' mine; I never cared for him, an' he could never stick me. It's not because he was Commandant of the Battalion that I was Quarther-Masther of, that we were friends.

MRS BOYLE. He's gone now—the Lord be good to him! God help his poor oul' creature of a mother, for no matther whose friend or enemy he was, he was her poor son.

BENTHAM. The whole thing is terrible, Mrs Boyle; but the only way to deal with a mad dog is to destroy him.

MRS BOYLE. An' to think of me forgettin' about him bein' brought to the church tonight, an' we singin' an' all, but it was well we hadn't the gramophone goin', anyhow.

BOYLE. Even if we had aself. We've nothin' to do with these things, one way or t'other. That's the Government's business, an' let them do what we're payin' them for doin'.

MRS BOYLE. I'd like to know how a body's not to mind these things; look at the way they're afther leavin' the people in this very house. Hasn't the whole house, nearly, been massacreed? There's young Dougherty's husband with his leg off; Mrs Travers that had her son blew up be a mine in Inchegeela, in Co. Cork; Mrs Mannin' that lost wan of her sons in an ambush a few weeks ago, an' now, poor Mrs Tancred's only child gone West with his body made a collandher of. Sure, if it's not our business, I don't know whose business it is.

BOYLE. Here, there, that's enough about them things; they don't affect us, an' we needn't give a damn. If they want a wake, well, let them have a wake. When I was a sailor, I was always resigned to meet with a wathery grave; an', if they want to be soldiers, well, there's no use o' them squealin' when they meet a soldier's fate.

JOXER (*lilting*) Let me like a soldier fall—me breast expandin' to th' ball!

MRS BOYLE. In wan way, she deserves all she got; for lately, she let th' Die-hards make an open house of th' place; an' for th' last couple of months, either when th' sun was risin' or when th' sun was settin' you had C.I.D. men burstin' into your room, assin' you where were you born, where were you christened, where were you married, an' where would you be buried!

JOHNNY (*tensely; he slipping out of the bed, going over to the fire and sitting down there*) For God's sake, let us have no more o' this talk.

MRS MADIGAN (*to change the subject*) What about Mr Boyle's song before we start th' gramophone?

MARY (*coming from the room* L, *with her hat and coat on*) Mother, Charlie and I are goin' out for a little sthroll.

MRS BOYLE. All right, darlin'.

BENTHAM (*getting his stick and hat, going out with Mary, by the door* R) We won't be long away, Mrs Boyle.

MRS MADIGAN. Gwan, Captain, gwan.

BOYLE. E-e-e-e-eh, I'd want to have a few more jars in me, before I'd be in fettle for singin'.

JOXER. Give us that poem you writ t'other day. (*To the rest*) Aw, it's a darlin' poem, a daarlin' poem.

MRS BOYLE. God bless us, is he startin' to write poetry!

BOYLE (*rising to his feet*) E-e-c-e-eh. (*He recites in an emotional, consequential manner the following verses*)

Shawn an' I were friends, sir, to me he was all in all.
His work was very heavy and his wages were very small.
None betther on th' beach as Docker, I'll go bail,
'Tis now I'm feelin' lonely, for today he lies in jail.
He was not what some call pious—seldom at church or prayer;
For the greatest scoundrels I know, sir, goes every Sunday there.
Fond of his pint—well, rather, but hated the Boss by creed
But never refused a copper to comfort a pal in need.

E-e-e-e-eh. (*He sits down*)

MRS MADIGAN. Grand, grand; you should folly that up, you should folly that up.

JOXER. It's a daarlin' poem!

BOYLE (*delightedly*) E-e-e-e-eh.

JOHNNY (*from his seat by the fire*) Are yous goin' to put on th' gramophone tonight, or are yous not?

MRS BOYLE. Gwan, Jack, put on a record.

MRS MADIGAN. Gwan, Captain, gwan.

BOYLE. Well, yous'll want to keep a dead silence.

(BOYLE *sets a record, starts the machine, and it begins to play "If you're Irish, come into the Parlour"*. (See note.)

As the tune is in full blare the door is suddenly opened by a brisk, little bald-headed man, dressed circumspectly in a black suit; he glares fiercely at all in the room; he is "NEEDLE" NUGENT, *a tailor. He carries his hat in his hand.* BOYLE *stops the gramophone*)

NUGENT (*loudly*) Are yous goin' to have that thing bawlin' an' the funeral of Mrs Tancred's son passin' the house? Have none of yous any respect for the Irish people's National regard for the dead?

MRS BOYLE. Maybe, Needle Nugent, it's nearly time we had a little less respect for the dead, an' a little more regard for the livin'.

MRS MADIGAN (*indignantly*) We don't want you, Mr Nugent, to teach us what we learned at our mother's knee. You don't look yourself as if you were dyin' of grief; if y'ass Maisie Madigan anything, I'd call you a real thrue Die-hard an' live-soft Republican, attendin' Republican funerals in the day, an' stopping up half the night makin' suits for the Civic Guards!

(*Persons are heard running down to the street, some saying,* "Here it is, here it is." NUGENT *withdraws by the door* R, *and the rest, except* JOHNNY, *go to the window above the door* R, *looking into the street, and look out. Sounds of a crowd coming nearer are heard; a portion are singing*)

To Jesus' Heart all burning
With fervent love for men,
My heart with fondest yearning
Shall raise its joyful strain.
While ages course along,
Blest be with loudest song,
The Sacred Heart of Jesus
By every heart and tongue.

MRS BOYLE. Here's the hearse, here's the hearse!

BOYLE. There's t'oul' mother walkin' behin' the coffin.

MRS MADIGAN. You can hardly see the coffin with the wreaths.

JOXER. Oh, it's a darlin' funeral, a daarlin' funeral!

MRS MADIGAN. We'd have a betther view from the street.

BOYLE (*coming away from the window, and going out by the door* R) Yes—this place ud give you a crick in your neck.

(*All, except* JOHNNY, *follow him out by the door* R.

JOHNNY, *taking no notice, sits moodily by the fire, gazing into it. After a few moments' pause, a young man in a trench coat, his cap, with a large peak, pulled down over his eyes, enters by the door* R. *He stands just inside the door, looking at* JOHNNY, *who doesn't know that he has entered*)

THE YOUNG MAN. Quarther-Masther Boyle.

JOHNNY (*turning round with a start*) The Mobilizer!

THE YOUNG MAN. You're not at the funeral?

JOHNNY. I'm not well.

THE YOUNG MAN (*coming to* C) I'm glad I've found you; you were stoppin' at your aunt's; I called there, but you'd gone. I've to give you an ordher to attend a Battalion Staff meetin' the night afther tomorrow.

JOHNNY. Where?

THE YOUNG MAN. I don't know; you're to meet me at the Pillar at eight o'clock; then we're to go to a place I'll be told of tonight; there we'll meet a mothor that'll bring us to the meetin'. They think you might be able to know somethin' about them that gave the bend where Commandant Tancred was shelterin'. (*He returns to the door* R, *and turns to listen to Johnny*)

JOHNNY. I'm not goin', then. I know nothing about Tancred.

THE YOUNG MAN (*at the door* R) You'd betther come for your own sake—remember your oath.

JOHNNY (*passionately*) I won't go! Haven't I done enough for Ireland! I've lost me arm, an' me hip's desthroyed so that I'll never be able to walk right agen! Good God, haven't I done enough for Ireland?

THE YOUNG MAN. Boyle, no man can do enough for Ireland.

(THE YOUNG MAN *goes out by the door* R.

Faintly in the distance the crowd is heard saying)

Hail, Mary, full of grace, the Lord is with Thee;
Blessed art Thou amongst women, and blessed, etc.

CURTAIN

ACT III

SCENE—*The same as Act II. It is about half-past six on a November evening.*

A bright fire is burning in the grate; MARY, *dressed to go out, is sitting on a chair by the fire, leaning forward, her hands under her chin, her elbows on her knees. A look of dejection, mingled with uncertain anxiety, is on her face. A lamp, turned low, is lighting on the table. The votive light under the picture of the Virgin gleams more redly than ever. It is two months later.* MRS BOYLE *is standing front of the table, looking anxiously at Mary.*

MRS BOYLE. An' has Bentham never even written to you since—not one line for the past month?

MARY (*tonelessly*) Not even a line, mother.

MRS BOYLE. That's very curious. . . . What came between the two of yous at all? To leave you so sudden, an' yous so great together. (*She goes back round* R *of the table, and takes up her coat and hat from the bed in the alcove*) To go away t' England, an' not to even leave you his address . . . The way he was always bringin' you to dances, I thought he was mad afther you. Are you sure you said nothin' to him?

MARY. No, mother—at least nothing that could possibly explain his givin' me up.

MRS BOYLE. You know you're a bit hasty at times, Mary, an' say things you shouldn't say.

MARY. I never said to him what I shouldn't say, I'm sure of that.

MRS BOYLE (*coming back to front of the table*) How are you sure of it?

MARY. Because I love him with all my heart and soul, mother. Why, I don't know; I often thought to myself that he wasn't the man poor Jerry was, but I couldn't help loving him, all the same.

MRS BOYLE. But you shouldn't be frettin' the way you are; when a woman loses a man, she never knows what she's afther losin', to be sure, but, then, she never knows what she's afther gainin', either. You're not the one girl of a month ago—you look like one pinin' away. It's long ago I had a right to bring you to the doctor, instead of waitin' till tonight.

MARY. There's no necessity, really, mother, to go to the doctor; nothing serious is wrong with me—I'm run down and disappointed, that's all.

MRS BOYLE. I'll not wait another minute; I don't like the look of you at all. . . . I'm afraid we made a mistake in throwin' over poor Jerry. . . . He'd have been betther for you than that Bentham.

MARY. Mother, the best man for a woman is the one for whom she has the most love, and Charlie had it all.

MRS BOYLE (*putting on her hat and coat*) Well, there's one thing to be said for him—he couldn't have been thinkin' of the money, or he wouldn't ha' left you . . . it must ha' been somethin' else.

MARY (*wearily*) I don't know . . . I don't know, mother . . . only I think . . .

MRS BOYLE. What d'ye think?

MARY. I imagine . . . he thought . . . we weren't . . . good enough for him.

MRS BOYLE (*indignantly*) An' what was he himself, only a school teacher? Though I don't blame him for fightin' shy of people like that Joxer fella an' that oul' Madigan wan—nice sort o' people for your father to inthroduce to a man like Mr Bentham. You might have told me all about this before now, Mary; I don't know why you like to hide everything from your mother; you knew Bentham, an' I'd ha' known nothin' about it if it hadn't bin for the Will; an' it was only today, afther long coaxin', that you let out that he'd left you.

MARY. It would have been useless to tell you—you wouldn't understand.

MRS BOYLE (*hurt*) Maybe not . . . Maybe I wouldn't understand . . . Well, we'll be off now. (*She crosses round the* R *end of the table and goes over to the door* L, *and speaks to Boyle inside the room* L) We're goin' now to the doctor's. Are you goin' to get up this evenin'?

BOYLE (*from inside the room* L) The pains in me legs is terrible! It's me should be poppin' off to the doctor instead o' Mary, the way I feel.

MRS BOYLE (*vigorously*) Sorra mend you! A nice way you were in last night—carried in in a frog's march, dead to the world. If that's the way you'll go on when you get the money it'll be the grave for you, an asylum for me and the Poorhouse for Johnny.

BOYLE (*irritably*) I thought you were goin'?

MRS BOYLE (*tartly*) That's what has you as you are—you can't bear to be spoken to. Knowin' the way we are, up to our ears in debt, it's a wondher you wouldn't ha' got up to go to th' solicitor's an' see if we could ha' gotten a little o' the money even.

BOYLE (*shouting*) I can't be goin' up there night, noon an' mornin', can I? He can't give the money till he gets it, can he? I can't get blood out of a turnip, can I?

MRS BOYLE. It's nearly two months since we heard of the Will, an' the money seems as far off as ever. . . . I suppose you know we owe twenty poun's to oul' Murphy?

BOYLE. I've a faint recollection of you tellin' me that before.

MRS BOYLE. Well, you'll go over to the shop yourself for the things in future—I'll face him no more.

BOYLE. I thought you said you were goin'?

MRS BOYLE. I'm goin' now; come on, Mary.

(MARY *goes over to the door* R, *where she waits dejectedly for Mrs Boyle.* MRS BOYLE *moves over to join her when she hears* BOYLE *shouting after her*)

BOYLE (*calling from the room* L) Ey, Juno, ey!

MRS BOYLE (*halted* C *behind the table*) Well, what d'ye want, now?

BOYLE (*inside the room* L) Is there e'er a bottle of stout left?

MRS BOYLE (*glancing at the chest of drawers*) There's two of them here, still.

BOYLE (*inside the room* L) Show us in one of them, an' leave t'other there till I get up. An' throw us in the paper that's on the table, an' the bottle of liniment that's in th' drawer.

(MRS BOYLE *goes over to the chest of drawers, takes a bottle of liniment from one of the drawers, comes down to the table, and picks up a paper*)

MRS BOYLE (*to Boyle inside the room* L) What paper is it you want—the *Catholic Herald*?

BOYLE (*calling contemptuously from the room* L) The *Catholic Herald*! The *News of the World*!

(MRS BOYLE *leaves down the paper she picked up, and picks up the other one from the table. She then brings the paper, bottle of stout and liniment in to Boyle, in the room* L, *and comes out again. She takes a second bottle of stout from the chest of drawers, and puts it on the centre of the table and goes over to the door* L *again*)

MRS BOYLE (*calling in to Boyle*) Mind the candle, now, an' don't burn the house over our heads. I left the other bottle of stout in the centre of the table.

(MRS BOYLE *crosses over, behind the table, to* MARY, *standing at the door* R, *and both go out by that door.*

A few moments' pause, and the loud popping of a cork is heard from inside the room L.

A pause! then outside the door is heard the voice of JOXER *lilting softly:* "Me pipe I'll smoke, as I dhrive me moke . . . are you . . . there . . . More . . . aar . . . i . . . tee!" *A gentle knock is heard and, after a pause, the door opens, and* JOXER, *followed by* NUGENT, *enters*)

JOXER. Be God, they must be all out; I was thinkin' there was somethin' up when he didn't answer the signal. We seen Juno an' Mary goin', but I didn't see him, an' it's very seldom he escapes me.

NUGENT. He's not goin' to escape me—he's not goin' to be let go to the fair altogether.

JOXER. Sure, the house couldn't hould them lately; an' he

goin' about like a mastherpiece of the Free State counthry; forgettin' their friends; forgettin' God—wouldn't even lift his hat passin' a chapel! Sure they were bound to get a dhrop! An' you really think there's no money comin' to him afther all?

NUGENT. Not as much as a red rex, man; I've been a bit anxious this long time over me money, an' I went up to the solicitor's to find out all I could—ah, man, they were goin' to throw me down the stairs. They toul' me that the oul' cock himself had the stairs worn away comin' up afther it, an' they black in the face tellin' him he'd get nothin'. Some way or another that the Will is writ he won't be entitled to get as much as a make!

JOXER. Ah, I thought there was somethin' curious about the whole thing; I've bin havin' sthrange dhreams for the last couple o' weeks. An' I notice that that Bentham fella doesn't be comin' here now—there must be somethin' on the mat there too. Anyhow, who in the name o' God ud leave anythin' to that oul' bummer? Sure it ud be unnatural. An' the way Juno an' him's been throwin' their weight about for the last few months! Ah, him that goes a borrowin' goes a sorrowin'!

NUGENT. Well, he's not goin' to throw his weight about in the suit I made for him much longer. I'm tellin' you seven poun' aren't to be found growin' on the bushes these days.

JOXER (*with virtuous indignation*) An' there isn't hardly a neighbour in the whole street that hasn't lent him money on the strength of what he was goin' to get, but they're after backing the wrong horse. Wasn't it a mercy o' God that I'd nothin' to give him! The softy I am, you know, I'd ha' lent him me last juice! (tuppence). I must have had somebody's good prayers. Ah, afther all, an honest man's the noblest work o' God!

(BOYLE *coughs inside.* NUGENT *and* JOXER *start and listen.* BOYLE *coughs again*)

Whisht, damn it, he must be inside in bed.

NUGENT. Inside o' bed or outside of it he's goin' to pay me for that suit, or give it back—he'll not climb up my back as easily as he thinks.

JOXER. Gwan in at wanst, man, an' get it off him, an' don't be a fool.

NUGENT (*crossing Joxer, and going to the door* L, *opening it and looking in*) Ah, don't disturb yourself, Mr Boyle; I hope you're not sick?

BOYLE (*inside the room* L) Th' oul' legs, Mr Nugent, the oul' legs.

NUGENT. I just called over to see if you could let me have anything off the suit?

BOYLE. E-e-e-eh, how much is this it is?

NUGENT. It's the same as it was at the start—seven poun's.

(JOXER *has been listening gleefully to the argument between Boyle and Nugent, as he stands behind the table* C. *He turns to look around the room, and catches sight of the bottle of stout on the table. His eyes are fixed on it for a few moments; then he looks round towards the door* L, *sees that* NUGENT *is busy speaking to Boyle, has his back turned to him. With rapid movements, he whips the stout from the table, and shoves it into his breast pocket, and assumes an innocent look*)

BOYLE (*from inside the room* L) I'm glad you kem, Mr Nugent; I want a good, heavy top-coat—Irish frieze, if you have it. How much would a top-coat like that be, now?

NUGENT. About six poun's.

BOYLE. Six poun's? (*He adds up*) Six an' seven . . . six an' seven . . . is thirteen—that'll be thirteen poun's I'll owe you.

(*A look of indignant stupefaction comes on* NUGENT'S *face. Then he dashes into the room* L, *and runs out again, with a suit over one arm. He stops outside the door* L *and looks back*)

NUGENT (*looking back into the room* L) You'll owe me no thirteen poun's. Maybe you think you're betther able to owe it than pay it.

BOYLE (*frantically—inside the room*) Here, come back to hell ower that! Where'r you goin' with them clothes of mine?

NUGENT. Where am I goin' with them clothes of yours? Well, I like your damn cheek!

BOYLE (*inside the room*) Here, what am I goin' to dhress meself in when I'm goin' out?

NUGENT. You can put yourself in a bolsther-cover, if you like.

(NUGENT *crosses to* R *behind the table, followed by* JOXER, *whom he passes* C)

JOXER (*ironically, as he follows Nugent*) What'll he dhress himself in! Gentleman Jack in his frieze coat.

BOYLE (*shouting from inside the room* L, *as Nugent and Joxer reach the door* R) Ey, Nugent; ey, Nugent, Mr Nugent, Mr Nugent!

(NUGENT *and* JOXER *go out by the door* R.

After a short pause, BOYLE *comes hurrying out of the room* L, *in shirt, trousers and socks. He runs rapidly across behind the table, to the door* R, *calling* "Ey, Mr Nugent." *He opens the door* R *and calls out again,* "Mr Nugent; ey, Mr Nugent." JOXER *suddenly meets him at the door, as if he had just come up*)

JOXER (*meeting him at the door*) What's up, what's wrong, Captain?

BOYLE (*frantically*) Nugent's been here an' took away me suit —the only things I had to go out in!

JOXER. Tuk your suit—for God's sake! An' what were you doin' while he was takin' them?

BOYLE (*moving from the door* R *to behind the table*) I was in bed when he stole in like a thief in the night, an' before I knew even what he was thinkin' of, he whipped them from the chair, an' was off like a redshank!

JOXER. An' what, in the name o' God, did he do that for?

BOYLE. What did he do it for? (*Fiercely*) How the hell do I know what he done it for?—jealousy an' spite, I suppose.

JOXER (R *of Boyle*) Did he not say what he done it for?

BOYLE. Amn't I afther tellin' you that he had them whipped up an' was gone before I could open me mouth?

JOXER. That was a very sudden thing to do; there mus' be somethin' behin' it. Did he hear anythin', I wondher?

BOYLE. Did he hear anythin'?—you talk very queer, Joxer—what could he hear?

JOXER. About you not gettin' the money, in some way or t'other?

BOYLE. An' what ud prevent me from gettin' th' money?

JOXER. That's jus' what I was thinkin'—what ud prevent you from gettin' the money—nothin', as far as I can see.

(BOYLE, *in a frenzied state of agitation, looks at the table, behind which he has moved, glances round at the chest of drawers, then back at the table with a concentrated look of bewilderment, till the fact that the bottle of stout which Mrs Boyle left on the table has disappeared.* JOXER *watches him with a look of pretended wonder*)

BOYLE (*with gaze concentrated on the table*) Aw, Holy God!

JOXER (*simulating surprise*) What's up, Jack?

BOYLE (*in a tone of fury mixed with resignation*) He must have afther lifted the bottle of stout that Juno left on the table!

JOXER (*pretending to be horrified*) Ah, no, ah, no; he wouldn't be afther doin' that now.

BOYLE (*angrily*) An' who done it, then? (*He points to the centre of the table*) Juno left a bottle of stout there, an' it's gone—it didn't walk away, did it? (*He shambles over from behind the table to the fire-place, a look of misery on his face*)

(JOXER *remains behind the table, a look of surprised sorrow on his face*)

JOXER. Oh, that's shockin'; oh, man's inhumanity to man makes countless thousands mourn.

(*The door* R *is suddenly opened, and* MRS MADIGAN, *excited and angry-looking, comes into the room*)

MRS MADIGAN (*with a note of sarcasm in her polite manner*) I hope I'm not disturbing you in any discussion on your forthcomin' legacy—if I may use the word—and that you'll let me have a barny for a minute or two with you, Mr Boyle.

BOYLE (*uneasily*) To be sure, Mrs Madigan—an oul' friend's always welcome.

Joxer. Come in the evenin', come in th' mornin'; come when you're assed, or come without warnin', Mrs Madigan.

Boyle. Sit down, Mrs Madigan.

Mrs Madigan (*ominously*) Th' few words I have to say can be said standin'. Puttin' aside all formularies, I suppose you remember me lendin' you some time ago three poun's that I raised on blankets an' furniture in me uncle's?

(Boyle *takes a little notebook from his trousers' pocket, passes over a few pages, then looks at a page in the book*)

Boyle. I remember it well. I have it recorded in me book—three poun's five shillin's from Maisie Madigan, raised on articles pawned; an', item: fourpence, given to make up the price of a pint, on th' principle that no bird ever flew on wan wing; all to be repaid at par, when the ship comes home.

Mrs Madigan (l) Well, ever since I shoved in the blankets I've been perishing with th' cowld, an' I've decided, if I'll be too hot in th' nex' world aself, I'm not goin' to be too cowld in this wan; an' consequently, I want me three poun's, if you please.

Boyle. This is a very sudden demand, Mrs Madigan, an' can't be met; but I'm willin' to give you a receipt in full, in full.

Mrs Madigan. Come on, out with th' money, an' don't be jack-actin'.

Boyle. You can't get blood out of a turnip, can you?

Mrs Madigan (*rushing over, across front of the table, catching Boyle by the shoulders and shaking him*) Gimme me money, y'oul' reprobate, or I'll shake the worth of it out of you!

Boyle. Ey, houl' on, there; houl' on, there! You'll wait for your money now, me lassie!

(Mrs Madigan *is wild with indignation. She looks venomously round the room; her eye lights on the gramophone standing on top of the chest of drawers. She thinks violently for a second. She rushes across behind the table, in front of* Joxer, *who goes back to avoid the rush, to the chest of drawers,* r *back, seizes the gramophone, comes down stage* l *to the door* l, *where she pauses to speak*)

Mrs Madigan (*as she seizes the gramophone*) I'll wait for it, will I? Well, I'll not wait long; if I can't get the cash, I'll get the worth of it.

Boyle (*to Mrs Madigan, when she seizes the gramophone*) Ey, ey, there, where'r you goin' with that?

Mrs Madigan. I'm goin' to th' pawn to get me three quid five shillin's; I'll brin' you th' ticket, an' then you can do what you like, me bucko.

Boyle. You can't touch that, you can't touch that! It's not my property, an' it's not ped for yet!

Mrs Madigan. So much th' betther. It'll be an ayse to me

conscience, for I'm takin' what doesn't belong to you. You're not goin' to be swankin' it like a paycock with Maisie Madigan's money—I'll pull some of the gorgeous feathers out of your tail!

(MRS MADIGAN, *carrying the gramophone in her arms, goes indignantly out by the door* R, *leaving* BOYLE *and* JOXER *gaping in astonishment. A short pause*)

BOYLE (*in utter perplexity*) What's th' world comin' to at all? I ass you, Joxer Daly, is there any morality left anywhere?

JOXER. I wouldn't ha' believed it, only I seen it with me own two eyes. I didn't think Maisie Madigan was that sort of a woman; she has either a sup taken, or she's heard somethin'.

BOYLE (*looking fixedly at Joxer*) Heard somethin'—about what, if it's not any harm to ass you?

JOXER. She must ha' heard some rumour or other that you weren't goin' to get th' money.

BOYLE. Who says I'm not goin' to get th' money?

JOXER. Sure, I know—I was only sayin'.

BOYLE (*coming from the fire over to Joxer, behind the table*) Only sayin' what?

JOXER. Nothin'.

BOYLE. You were goin' to say somethin', don't be a twisther.

JOXER (*angrily*) Who's a twisther?

BOYLE. Why don't you speak your mind, then?

JOXER. You never twisted yourself—no, you wouldn't know how!

BOYLE (*shouting*) Did you ever know me to twist; did you ever know me to twist?

JOXER (*fiercely*) Did you ever do anythin' else! Sure, you can't believe a word that comes out o' your mouth.

BOYLE (*violently*) Here, get out, ower o' this; I always knew you were a prognosticator an' a procrastinator!

JOXER (*going out by the door* R, *as Johnny comes in by the door* L) The anchor's weighed, farewell, ree . . . mem . . . ber . . . me. Jacky Boyle, Esquire, infernal rogue an' damned liar!

JOHNNY. Joxer an' you at it agen?—when are you goin' to have a little respect for yourself, an' not be always makin' a show of us all? (*He sits down moodily in the chair by the fire*)

BOYLE. Are you goin' to lecture me now?

JOHNNY. Is mother back from the doctor yet, with Mary?

(*After a short pause,* MRS BOYLE *enters by the door* R. *By the serious look on her face, it is clear that something has happened. She goes, by the* R *end of the table, to the alcove, dragging her feet along in a weary way, and takes off her coat without a word. There is a peculiar silence felt, till* BOYLE *speaks. She keeps her hat on*)

BOYLE. Well, what did the docthor say about Mary?

(MRS BOYLE *comes down stage* R, *brings a chair to front* R *end of the table, points to another chair, front* L *end of the table, as she sits down on the chair* R, *and speaks to Boyle*)

MRS BOYLE (*with suppressed agitation*) Sit down there, Jack; I've something to say to you . . . about Mary.

(BOYLE, *surprised and a little frightened, sits on the chair,* L *end of the table. He shows by his look that he feels something's wrong*)

BOYLE. About . . . Mary . . . More throuble in our native land. Well, what is it?

MRS BOYLE. It's about Mary.

BOYLE. Well, what about Mary—there's nothin' wrong with her, is there?

MRS BOYLE. I'm sorry to say there's a gradle wrong with her.

BOYLE. A gradle wrong with her! (*Peevishly*) First Johnny an' now Mary; is the whole house goin' to become an hospital! It's not consumption, is it?

MRS BOYLE. No . . . it's not consumption . . . it's worse.

JOHNNY. Worse! Well, we'll have to get her into some place ower this, there's no one here to mind her.

MRS BOYLE. We'll all have to mind her now. You might as well know now, Johnny, as another time. (*To Boyle*) D'ye know what the doctor said to me about her, Jack?

BOYLE. How ud I know—I wasn't there, was I?

MRS BOYLE. He told me to get her married at wanst.

BOYLE. Married at wanst! An' why did he say the like o' that?

MRS BOYLE. Because Mary's goin' to have a baby in a short time.

BOYLE (*panic-stricken*) Goin' to have a baby!—my God, what'll Bentham say when he hears that?

MRS BOYLE. Are you blind, man, that you can't see that it was Bentham that has done this wrong to her?

BOYLE (*passionately*) Then he'll marry her, he'll have to marry her!

MRS BOYLE. You know he's gone to England, an' God knows where he is now.

(BOYLE *jumps from his chair in a frenzy of rage, and goes round* R *end of the table to the back, where he clenches his fists, and shows the mood of rage which dominates him*)

BOYLE. I'll folly him, I'll folly him, an' bring him back, an' make him do her justice. The scoundrel, I might ha' known what he was, with his yogees an' his prawna!

MRS BOYLE. We'll have to keep it quiet till we see what we can do.

BOYLE. Oh, isn't this a nice thing to come on top o' me, an' the state I'm in! A pretty show I'll be to Joxer an' to that oul' wan, Madigan! Amn't I afther goin' through enough without havin' to go through this!

MRS BOYLE. What you an' I'll have to go through'll be nothin' to what poor Mary'll have to go through; for you an' me is middlin' old, an' most of our years is spent; but Mary'll have maybe forty years to face an' handle, an' every wan of them'll be tainted with a bitther memory.

BOYLE (*vengefully*) Where is she? Where is she till I tell her off? I'm tellin' you when I'm done with her she'll be a sorry girl!

MRS BOYLE. I left her in me sisther's till I came to speak to you. You'll say nothin' to her, Jack; ever since she left school she's earned her livin', an' your fatherly care never throubled the poor girl.

BOYLE. Gwan, take her part agen her father! But I'll let you see whether I'll say nothin' to her or no! Her an' her readin'! That's more o' th' blasted nonsense that has the house fallin' down on top of us! What did th' likes of her, born in a tenement house, want with readin'? Her readin's afther bringin' her to a nice pass—oh, it's madnin', madnin', madnin'!

MRS BOYLE. When she comes back say nothin' to her, Jack, or she'll leave this place.

BOYLE. Leave this place! Ay, she'll leave this place, an' quick too!

MRS BOYLE. If Mary goes, I'll go with her.

BOYLE (*roughly*) Well, go with her! Well, go, th' pair o' yous! I lived before I seen yous, an' I can live when yous are gone. Isn't this a nice thing to come rollin' in on top o' me afther all your prayin' to St Anthony an' The Little Flower. An' she's a child o' Mary, too—I wonder what'll the nuns think of her now? An' it'll be bellows'd all over th' disthrict before you could say Jack Robinson; an' whenever I'm seen they'll whisper, "That's th' father of Mary Boyle that had th' kid be th' swank she used to go with; d'ye know, d'ye know?" To be sure they'll know--more about it than I will meself!

JOHNNY (*viciously*) She should be dhriven out o' th' house she's brought disgrace on!

MRS BOYLE (*turning to Johnny*) Hush, you, Johnny. (*Turning to Boyle*) We needn't let it be bellows'd all over the place; all we've got to do is to leave this place quietly an' go somewhere where we're not known, an' nobody'll be th' wiser.

BOYLE. You're talkin' like a two-year-oul', woman. Where'll we get a place ou' o' this?—places aren't that easily got.

MRS BOYLE. But, Jack, when we get the money . . .

BOYLE (*stopping his walk behind the table to look intently at Mrs Boyle*) Money—what money?

MRS BOYLE. Why, oul' Ellison's money, of course.

BOYLE. There's no money comin' from oul' Ellison, or anyone

else. Since you've heard of wan throuble, you might as well hear of another. There's no money comin' to us at all—the Will's a washout!

MRS BOYLE (*stupefied*) What are you sayin', man—no money?

JOHNNY. How could it be a washout?

BOYLE. The boyo that's afther doin' it to Mary done it to me as well. The thick made out the Will wrong; he said in th' Will, only first cousin an' second cousin, instead of mentionin' our names, an' now anyone that thinks he's a first cousin or second cousin t'oul' Ellison can claim the money as well as me, an' they're springin' up in hundreds, an' comin' from America an' Australia, thinkin' to get their whack out of it, while all the time the lawyers is gobblin' it up, till there's not as much as ud buy a stockin' for your lovely daughter's baby!

MRS BOYLE (*vehemently*) I don't believe it, I don't believe it, I don't believe it!

JOHNNY (*angrily to Boyle*) Why did you say nothin' about this before?

MRS BOYLE (*appealingly*) You're not serious, Jack; you're not serious!

BOYLE. I'm tellin' you the scholar, Bentham, made a banjax o' th' Will; instead o' sayin', "th' rest o' me property to be divided between me first cousin, Jack Boyle, an' me second cousin, Mick Finnegan, o' Santhry", he writ down only, "me first an' second cousins", an' the world an' his wife are afther th' property now.

MRS BOYLE. Now, I know why Bentham left poor Mary in th' lurch; I can see it all now—oh, is there not even a middlin' honest man left in th' world?

JOHNNY (*fiercely to Boyle*) An' you let us run into debt, an' borreyed money from everybody to fill yourself with beer! An' now, you tell us the whole thing's a washout! Oh, if it's thrue, I'm done with you, for you're worse than me sisther Mary!

BOYLE (*threateningly, and moving over by the table, to Johnny*) You hole your tongue, d'ye hear? I'll not take any lip from you. Go an' get Bentham if you want satisfaction for all that's afther happenin' us.

JOHNNY. I won't hole me tongue, I won't hole me tongue! I'll tell you what I think of you, father an' all as you are . . . you . . .

MRS BOYLE (*appealing to Johnny*) Johnny, Johnny, Johnny, for God's sake, be quiet!

JOHNNY. I'll not be quiet, I'll not be quiet; he's a nice father, isn't he? Is it any wondher Mary went asthray, when . . .

MRS BOYLE. Johnny, Johnny, for my sake be quiet—for your mother's sake!

BOYLE. I'm goin' out now to have a few dhrinks with th' last few makes I have, an' tell that lassie o' yours not to be here when I come back: for if I lay me eyes on her, I'll lay me han's on her.

an' if I lay me han's on her, I won't be accountable for me actions!

JOHNNY. Take care somebody doesn't lay his han's on you—y'oul' . . .

MRS BOYLE. Johnny, Johnny!

BOYLE (*at the door, about to go out*) Oh, a nice son, an' a nicer daughter, I have. (*He calls loudly upstairs*) Joxer, Joxer, are you there?

JOXER (*from a distance*) I'm here, More . . . ee . . . aar . . . i . . . tee!

BOYLE. I'm goin' down to Foley's—are you comin'?

JOXER. Come with you? With that sweet call me heart is stirred; I'm only waiting for the word, an' I'll be with you, like a bird!

(BOYLE *and* JOXER *pass the door going out*)

JOHNNY (*throwing himself on the bed*) I've a nice sisther, an' a nice father, there's no bettin' on it. I wish to God a bullet or a bomb had whipped me ou' o' this long ago! Not one o' yous, not one o' yous, have any thought for me!

MRS BOYLE (*with passionate remonstrance*) If you don't whisht, Johnny, you'll drive me mad. Who has kep' th' home together for the past few years—only me. An' who'll have to bear th' biggest part o' this throuble but me—but whinin' an' whingin' isn't goin' to do any good.

JOHNNY. You're to blame yourself for a gradle of it—givin' him his own way in everything, an' never assin' to check him, no matther what he done. Why didn't you look afther th' money? why . . .

(*A knock at the door* R. MRS BOYLE *takes no notice, but sits on her chair in despair. The knock again, louder.* MRS BOYLE *gets up heavily from the chair, crosses front of the table, to the door* R, *and opens it. The two* FURNITURE-REMOVAL MEN, *wearing green baize aprons, enter, and stand to* R *of Mrs Boyle.* JOHNNY *turns on his seat to see who has come in, and listens to what is said*)

FIRST MAN. We've been sent up be th' Manager of the Hibernian Furnishing Co., Mrs Boyle, to take back the furniture that was got a while ago.

MRS BOYLE. Yous'll touch nothin' here—how do I know who yous are?

FIRST MAN (*showing a paper*) There's the ordher, ma'am. (*He reads*) A chest o' drawers, a table, wan easy an' two ordinary chairs; wan mirror; wan chestherfield divan, an' a wardrobe vase. (*He turns to his mate*) Come on, Bill, it's afther knockin'-off time, already. We'll the chest o' drawers first.

(*The two* MEN *cross* MRS BOYLE *near the door* R, *and go to the back* R. *Each takes an end of the chest of drawers. and carries it out by the door* R. MRS BOYLE *returns to front of the table and watches them*)

JOHNNY. For God's sake, mother, run down to Foley's an' bring father back, or we'll be left without a stick.

(*The* MEN *carry out the table*)

MRS BOYLE. What good would it be—you heard what he said before he went out.

JOHNNY. Can't you thry; he ought to be here, an' the like of this goin' on.

(MRS BOYLE *goes by the* L *end of the table to the alcove, takes her coat from the bed, puts it slowly on, comes down stage by the* R *end of the table, to the door* R. *As she reaches the door,* MARY *enters, tired and dejected. She runs to Mrs Boyle and puts her arms round her*)

MARY. What's up, mother? I met men carrying away the chest of drawers, an' everybody's talkin' about us not getting the money, after all.

MRS BOYLE (*near the door* R, *on Mary's* L) Everything's gone wrong, Mary. We're not gettin' a penny out of the Will, not a penny. I'll tell you all when I come back—I'm goin' to look for your father.

(MRS BOYLE *goes out by the door* R.

MARY, *with her head bent, crosses front of the table, to the chair that Boyle had occupied,* L *end of the table, and sits down on it.* JOHNNY *standing, leaning his elbow on the mantelpiece, watches her with a scornful look on his face*)

JOHNNY (*bitterly*) It's wondher you're not ashamed to show your face here, afther what has happened.

(JERRY *enters the door* R, *a look of hope on his face. He pauses by the door for a second, looks over at Mary, then comes closer, front of the table*)

JERRY (*softly*) Mary!

(MARY *does not answer, and sits silently on the chair*)

Mary, I want to speak to you for a few moments, may I?

(MARY *remains silent.*

JOHNNY *goes slowly into the room* L.

JERRY *crosses slowly, front of the table to Mary, and stands on her* R)

Your mother has told me everything, Mary, and I have come to you . . . I have come to tell you, Mary, that my love for you is greater and deeper than ever . . .

MARY (*with a sob*) Oh, Jerry, Jerry, say no more; all that is over now; anything like that is impossible now!

JERRY. Impossible? Why do you talk like that, Mary?

MARY. After all that has happened.

JERRY. What does it matter what has happened? We are young enough to be able to forget all those things. (*He catches her hand*) Mary, Mary, I am pleading for your love. With Labour, Mary, humanity is above everything; we are the Leaders in the fight for a new life. I want to forget Bentham, I want to forget that you left me—even for a while.

MARY. Oh, Jerry, Jerry, you haven't the bitter word of scorn for me after all.

JERRY (*passionately*) Scorn! I love you, love you, Mary!

MARY (*rising, and looking him in the eyes*) Even though . . .

(MARY *rises from the chair and turns to face* JERRY; *he takes her hand, and she looks up into his eyes*)

Even though . . .

JERRY. Even though you threw me over for another man; even though you gave me many a bitter word!

MARY. Yes, yes, I know; but you love me, even though . . . even though . . . I'm . . . goin' . . . goin' . . .

(JERRY *looks at her questioningly, and fear gathers in his eyes*)

Ah, I was thinkin' so. . . . You don't know everything!

JERRY (*poignantly*) Surely to God, Mary, you don't mean that . . . that . . . that . . .

MARY. Now you know all, Jerry; now you know all!

JERRY. My God, Mary, have you fallen as low as that?

MARY. Yes, Jerry, as you say, I have fallen as low as that.

(JERRY *moves a little away from her, to the* R. *He wishes to get away, but finds it awkward. He turns towards her again*)

JERRY. I didn't mean it that way, Mary . . . it came on me so sudden, that I didn't mind what I was sayin' . . . I never expected this—your mother never told me . . . I'm sorry . . . God knows, I'm sorry for you, Mary.

MARY. Let us say no more, Jerry; I don't blame you for thinkin' it's terrible . . . I suppose it is . . . Everybody'll think the same . . . it's only as I expected—your humanity is just as narrow as the humanity of the others.

JERRY (*half-way to the door* R) I'm sorry, all the same . . . I shouldn't have throubled you . . . I wouldn't had I known . . . (*He crosses on to the door* R) If I can ever do anything for you . . . Mary . . . I will.

(JERRY *pauses for a few moments at the door* R, *then goes quietly out. Another short pause, and* JOHNNY *returns slowly from the room* L, *comes to the fireplace, leans his arm on the mantelpiece, and looks down at* Mary. MARY *sinks down into the chair again*)

JOHNNY (*inquiringly*) Is he gone?
MARY (*tonelessly*) Yes.

(*The two* FURNITURE-REMOVAL MEN *re-enter by the door* R. *Each takes a chair*)

FIRST MAN (*apologetically*) Sorry, miss, but we have to live as well as the next man.

(*They carry out the table*)

JOHNNY. Isn't this terrible? I suppose you told him everything. Couldn't you have waited for a few days . . . He'd have stopped the taking of the things, if you'd kept your mouth shut. Are you burning to tell everyone of the shame you've brought on us?
MARY (*in agony*) Oh, this is unbearable!

(MARY *swiftly crosses to the door* R, *and goes out.*
The two FURNITURE-REMOVAL MEN *re-enter by the door* R)

FIRST MAN. We'll take the sofa, now.

(*They go to the sofa; the Votive Light flickers for a moment, and then goes out*)

JOHNNY (*glancing up at the light*) Mother of God, the light's gone out!
FIRST MAN (*startled*) You put the wind up me, the way you bawled that time. (*He goes over to the fireplace and peers down into the red bowl*) The oil's all gone, that's all. (*He goes back to help the other man with the sofa*)

(JOHNNY *gives an agonizing cry*)

JOHNNY. Mother of God, there's a shot I'm afther getting!

(*The* FIRST MAN *goes over towards Johnny, and looks at him anxiously*)

FIRST MAN. What's wrong with you, man—is it a fit you're afther takin'?
JOHNNY (*with a wail*) I'm afther feelin' a pain in me breast, like the tearin' by of a bullet.
FIRST MAN (*turning to his mate*) That chap's goin' mad—it's a wondher they'd leave a chap like that here be himself.

(*The door* R *suddenly flies open, and the two* IRREGULARS *enter swiftly. They carry revolvers in their hands. One crosses swiftly to Johnny; the other, standing in front of the two* FURNITURE-REMOVAL MEN, *covers them with his gun. They put their hands above their heads*)

FIRST IRREGULAR (*to the Furniture-Removal Men, quietly, quickly, and decisively*) Who are you—what are yous doin' here—quick!
FIRST FURNITURE-REMOVAL MAN (*in fear, answering rapidly*) Removin' furniture that's not paid for.

FIRST IRREGULAR. Get over to the other end of room; turn faces to wall, an' keep your hands up—quick!

(*The two* FURNITURE-REMOVAL MEN *turn, with hands over head, walk to the end of the room* C *back, and, with faces to the wall, stand there with hands over heads. The* FIRST IRREGULAR *then goes over to the other* IRREGULAR, *who is standing over Johnny at the fireplace*)

SECOND IRREGULAR (*to Johnny*) Come on, Shean Boyle, you're wanted; some of us have a word to say to you.

JOHNNY (*plaintively*) I'm sick; I can't; what do you want with me?

SECOND IRREGULAR (*catching one of Johnny's arms*) Come on, come on; we've a distance to go, an' we haven't much time—come on.

JOHNNY (*with pathetic appeal*) I'm an oul' comrade—yous wouldn't shoot an oul' comrade.

SECOND IRREGULAR. Poor Tancred was an oul' comrade o' yours, but you didn't think o' that when you gave him away to the gang that sent him to his grave. But we've no time to waste; come on—here, Dermot, ketch his arm.

(*The* IRREGULARS *pull* JOHNNY *from the chair, and drag him across the stage to front* C. *He feebly resists them*)

FIRST IRREGULAR (*suddenly to Johnny*) Have you your beads?

JOHNNY (*in a sweat of fear*) Me beads! Why do you ass me that, why do you ass me that?

SECOND IRREGULAR. Go on, go on, march!

JOHNNY. Are yous goin' to do in a comrade—look at me arm, I lost it for Ireland.

SECOND IRREGULAR. Commandant Tancred lost his life for Ireland.

JOHNNY (*praying as he is dragged along*) Sacred Heart of Jesus, have mercy on me! Mother o' God, pray for me—be with me now in the agonies o' death! . . . Hail, Mary, full o' grace . . . the Lord is . . . with Thee.

(*They drag out* JOHNNY BOYLE *by the door* R, *and the* CURTAIN *falls.*

When it rises again most of the furniture is gone. MARY *and* MRS BOYLE, *one on each side, are sitting in a darkened room, by the fire, on two boxes, for all the chairs are gone; it is an hour later*)

MRS BOYLE. I'll not wait much longer . . . what did they bring him away in the mothor for? Nugent says he thinks they had guns . . . is me throubles never goin' to be over? . . . If anything ud happen to poor Johnny, I think I'd lose me mind. (*Decisively*) I'll go to the Police Station, surely they ought to be able to do somethin'. (*She goes over to the alcove, back* L, *and takes her hat from the bed, and puts it on*)

(*Outside of the door* R, *voices are heard speaking*)

Whisht, is that something? Maybe, it's your father, though when I left him in Foley's he was hardly able to lift his head. Whisht!

(*A knock at the door* R, *and the voice of* Mrs Madigan *speaking very softly outside*)

Mrs Madigan. Mrs Boyle, Mrs Boyle.

(Mrs Boyle *from the alcove, crosses down to the door* R, *opens it, and* Mrs Madigan *comes in. She goes over to Mrs Boyle with an air of deep sympathy. They stand* RC, Mrs Madigan *on Mrs Boyle's* R. Mary *turns round to listen, but still sits on the box by the fire*)

Oh, Mrs Boyle, God an' His Blessed Mother be with you this night!

Mrs Boyle (*calmly*) What is it, Mrs Madigan? It's Johnny—something about Johnny.

Mrs Madigan. God send it's not, God send it's not Johnny!

Mrs Boyle. Don't keep me waitin', Mrs Madigan; I've gone through so much lately that I feel able for anything.

Mrs Madigan. Two polismen below wantin' you.

Mrs Boyle (*surprised*) Wantin' me; an' why do they want me?

Mrs Madigan. Some poor fella's been found, an' they think it's . . . it's . . .

Mrs Boyle (*with grief*) Johnny, Johnny!

Mary (*rushing from her place to Mrs Boyle and putting her arms round her*) Oh, mother, mother, me poor darlin' mother.

Mrs Boyle. Hush, hush, darlin'; you'll shortly have your own throuble to bear. (*To Mrs Madigan*) An' why do the polis think it's Johnny, Mrs Madigan?

Mrs Madigan. Because one o' the doctors knew him when he was attendin' with his poor arm.

Mrs Boyle. Oh, it's thrue, then; it's Johnny, it's me son, me own son!

Mary (*wildly*) Oh, it's thrue, it's thrue what Jerry Devine says—there isn't a God, there isn't a God; if there was He wouldn't let these things happen!

Mrs Boyle (*soothingly*) Mary, Mary, you mustn't say them things. We'll want all the help we can get from God an' His Blessed Mother now! These things have nothin' to do with the Will o' God. Ah, what can God do agen the stupidity o' men!

Mrs Madigan. The polis want you to go with them to the hospital to see the poor body—they're waitin' below.

Mrs Boyle. We'll go. Come, Mary, an' we'll never come back here agen. Let your father furrage for himself now; I've done all I could an' it was all no use—he'll be hopeless till the end of his days. I've got a little room in me sisther's where we'll stop till your throuble is over, an' then we'll work together for the sake of the baby.

MARY. My poor little child that'll have no father!

MRS BOYLE. It'll have what's far betther—it'll have two mothers.

(MRS BOYLE *releases herself gently from Mary, goes back to the alcove, takes her coat from the bed, and puts it on her.* MRS MADIGAN *goes to Mary, and puts an arm round her. A rough voice is heard shouting from outside the door* R)

VOICE (*outside the door* R) Are yous goin' to keep us waitin' for yous all night?

(MRS MADIGAN *runs to the door* R, *opens it, and shouts out*)

MRS MADIGAN. Take your hour, there, take your hour! If yous are in such a hurry, skip off, then, for nobody wants you here—if they did yous wouldn't be found. For you're the same as yous were undher the British Government—never where yous are wanted! As far as I can see, the Polis as Polis, in this city, is Null an' Void!

MRS BOYLE. We'll go, Mary, we'll go; you to see your poor dead brother, an' me to see me poor dead son!

MARY. I dhread it, mother, I dhread it!

(MRS MADIGAN *goes back to Mary, and again puts a sheltering arm round her. They stand a little in from the door* R. MRS BOYLE *comes slowly down to the centre of the stage, and stands there*)

MRS BOYLE. I forgot, Mary, I forgot; your poor oul' selfish mother was only thinkin' of herself. No, no, you mustn't come—it wouldn't be good for you. You go on to me sisther's an' I'll face th' ordeal meself. Maybe I didn't feel sorry enough for Mrs Tancred when her poor son was found as Johnny's been found now—because he was a Die-hard! (*With deep feeling*) Ah, why didn't I remember that then he wasn't a Die-hard or a Stater, but only a poor dead son! It's well I remember all that she said—an' it's my turn to say it now: What was the pain I suffered, Johnny, bringin' you into the world to carry you to your cradle to the pains I'll suffer carryin' you out o' the world to bring you to your grave! Mother o' God, Mother o' God, have pity on us all! Blessed Virgin, where were you when me darlin' son was riddled with bullets, when me darlin' son was riddled with bullets? Sacred Heart o' Jesus, take away our hearts o' stone, and give us hearts o' flesh! Take away this murdherin' hate, an' give us Thine own eternal love!

(MRS BOYLE *crosses by in front of Mrs Madigan and Mary, and goes slowly out by the door* R, *followed slowly by* MRS MADIGAN *and* MARY.

There is a pause, then the sound of shuffling steps are heard outside the door R. *The door opens and* BOYLE, *very drunk, enters, and shuffles across to* C. *He stands there for a few moments. Then* JOXER, *as drunk as Boyle, appears at the door, and supports himself against one side of it*)

BOYLE. I'm able to go no farther . . . Two polis, ey? . . . what were they doin' here, I wondher? . . . Up to no good, anyhow . . . an' Juno an' that lovely daughter o' mine with them. (*He takes a sixpence from his pocket and looks at it*) Wan single, solithary tanner left out of all I borreyed . . . (*He lets it fall*) The last o' the Mohicans. . . . The blinds is down, Joxer, the blinds is down!

JOXER (*walking unsteadily across the room, and anchoring at the bed*) Put all . . . your throubles . . . in your oul' kit bag . . . an' smile . . . smile . . . smile!

(BOYLE *staggers over to the* L, *and swayingly sits down on a box above the fireplace*)

BOYLE. The counthry'll have to steady itself . . . it's goin' . . . to hell . . . Where'r all . . . the chairs . . . gone to . . . steady itself, Joxer. (*In a hazy way, he notices the chairs are gone*) Chairs'll . . . have to . . . steady themselves . . . No matther . . . what anyone may . . . say. . . . Irelan' sober . . . is Irelan' . . . free.

JOXER (*stretching himself on the bed*) Chains . . . an' . . . slavaree . . . that's a darlin' motto . . . a daarlin' . . . motto!

BOYLE. If th' worst comes . . . to th' worse . . . I can join a . . . flyin' . . . column . . . I done . . . me bit . . . in Easther Week . . . had no business . . . to . . . be . . . there . . . but Captain Boyle's Captain Boyle!

JOXER. Breathes there a man with soul . . . so . . . de . . ad . . . this . . . me . . . o . . . wn, me nat . . . ive! . . . an'!

BOYLE (*subsiding into a sitting posture on the floor, stretching out his arms*) Commandant Kelly died . . . in them . . . arms . . . Joxer . . . Tell me Volunteer Butties . . . says he . . . that . . . I died for . . . Irelan'!

JOXER. D'jever rade Willie . . . Reilly . . . an' his . . . own . . . Colleen . . . Bawn? It's a darlin' story, a daarlin' story!

BOYLE. I'm telling you . . . Joxer . . . th' whole worl's . . . in a terr . . . ible state o' . . . chassis!

CURTAIN

BOYLE's *song, as he cooks breakfast*

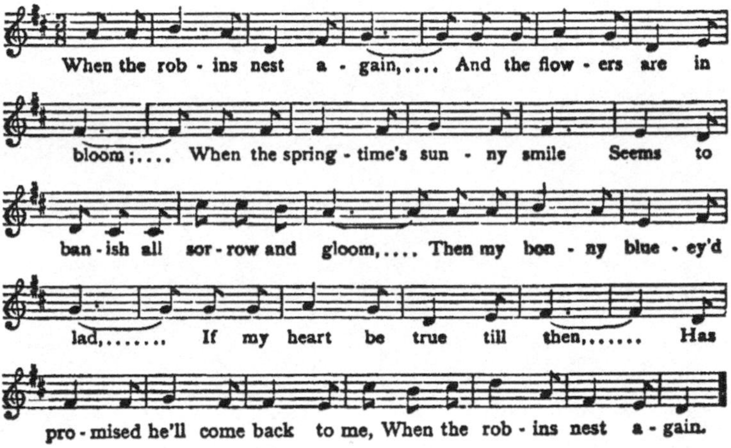
When the rob - ins nest a - gain, ... And the flow - ers are in
bloom ; . . . . When the spring - time's sun - ny smile Seems to
ban - ish all sor - row and gloom, ... Then my bon - ny blue - ey'd
lad, ... If my heart be true till then, ... Has
pro - mised he'll come back to me, When the rob - ins nest a - gain.

Sung by BOYLE, *end of Act I*

O my dar - ling Ju - no, I will be true to thee ; My
own, my dar - ling Ju - no, You're all the world to me.

PROPERTY AND FURNITURE PLOT

ACT I

Dresser with Delft
Blue and white coloured chalk statue of Blessed Virgin
Small crimson bowl for votive light
Kitchen table and two or three kitchen chairs
An old armchair
Teapot, frying-pan, cups and saucers, plates
Small mirror
Long-handled shovel
Newspaper
Three books
Fillet of ribbon for MARY
Document as Will for BENTHAM
Parcel of sausages for MRS BOYLE
Old lace curtains for window, back

ACT II

Gaudily upholstered couch or sofa
Three chairs upholstered in the same way
Highly polished chest of drawers
China ware for tea on chest of drawers
Bottle of whisky
Several bottles of stout
A cake, or several small ones
Big gaudy vase
Attaché-case, in which are writing materials
Fountain pen for BOYLE
Gramophone with some records
Bunch of artificial flowers for vase
Money in notes for JOXER
Silver coins for BOYLE
Coloured Christmas paper chains to hang under ceiling
Red bowl for light, as in Act I
A picture

ACT III

Same as Act I, with *Catholic Herald* or *Catholic Fireside*
Two revolvers for IRREGULARS
Silver coin, like a sixpence, for BOYLE
Two old boxes
Lamp
Suit of clothes for "NEEDLE" NUGENT
Bottle of liniment
Two newspapers

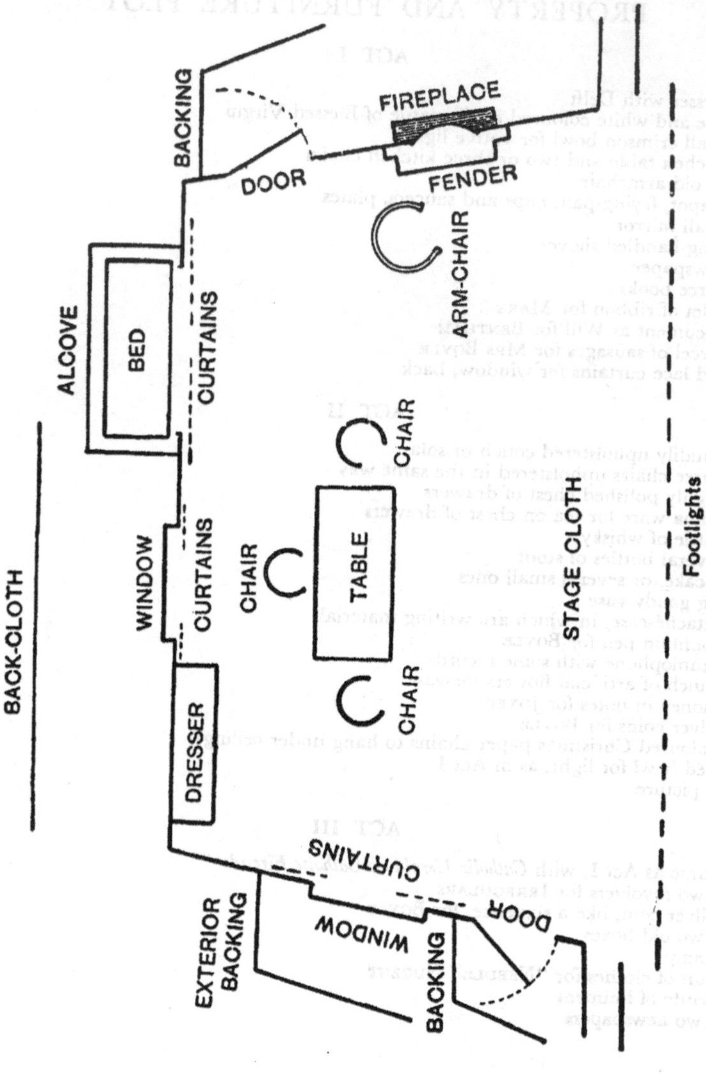
BACKING
FIREPLACE
DOOR
FENDER
ARM-CHAIR
ALCOVE
BED
CURTAINS
CHAIR
WINDOW
CURTAINS
CHAIR
TABLE
STAGE CLOTH
Footlights
CHAIR
BACK-CLOTH
DRESSER
CURTAINS
DOOR
WINDOW
EXTERIOR BACKING
BACKING

ACT I (SCENE 1)

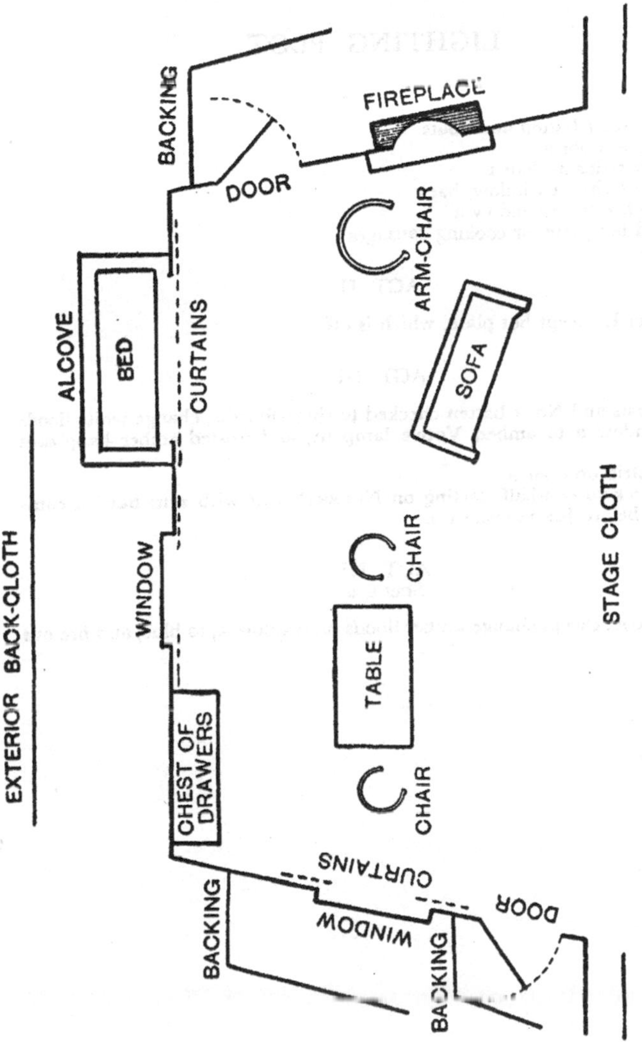

ACT II

Vase of flowers on chest of drawers. Lamp on table RC

LIGHTING PLOT

ACT 1

Full white No. 1 batten and floats
White strip at door R
Two amber strips at door L
Two amber strips at window, back
Two white floods on window R
Fire lit and hot plate for cooking sausages

ACT II

Same as Act I, except hot plate, which is off

ACT III

Open to floats and No. 1 batten checked to three-fourths, change white floods on window R to amber, Votive lamp lit, and frosted amber baby spot on it.
Knock off strip on door R
Further check to one-half starting on NUGENT's exit with suit; have it completed before JUNO's entrance.

ACT III
SCENE 2

Same as above, except change amber floods on window R, to blue, and fire out